THE BLOCKCHAIN FUTURE

BITCOIN, CRYPTOCURRENCY, BLOCKCHAIN TECHNOLOGY, DE-CENTRALISED LEDGERS, SMART CONTRACTS, CRYPTO WALLETS, NFTS AND WEB 3.0. WHAT IT CAN DO IN THE REAL WORLD NOW AND IN THE FUTURE.

ROBERT B. SEYMOUR

© **Copyright 2021 - All rights reserved.**

The content contained within this book may not be reproduced, duplicated, or transmitted without direct written permission from the author or the publisher.

Under no circumstances will any blame or legal responsibility be held against the publisher, or author, for any damages, reparation, or monetary loss due to the information contained within this book, either directly or indirectly.

Legal Notice:

This book is copyright protected. It is only for personal use. You cannot amend, distribute, sell, use, quote, or paraphrase any part, or the content within this book, without the author or publisher's permission.

Disclaimer Notice:

Please note that the information contained within this document is for educational and entertainment purposes only. All effort has been executed to present accurate, up-to-date, reliable, complete information. No warranties of any kind are declared or implied. Readers acknowledge that the author is not rendering legal, financial, medical, or professional advice. The content within this book has been derived from various sources. Please consult a licensed professional before attempting any techniques outlined in this book.

By reading this document, the reader agrees that under no circumstances is the author responsible for any losses, direct or indirect, that are incurred due to the use of the information in this document, including, but not limited to, errors, omissions, or inaccuracies.

ABOUT THE AUTHOR

After spending 20 years as CEO of businesses in the telecoms, mobile and the WiFi marketing space, my 'love' of technology brought my attention to Blockchain technology and Cryptocurrency. With my business experience I thought it would be very straightforward! Hell, no!

After researching the opportunities that Blockchain will underpin in our everyday lives, I decided to write this book. I have continued my research for the last year and I am convinced that the new Blockchain technology will change people's life and work dynamics dramatically.

I would like the reader that wants to explore this new area of technology to have a simple understanding and a starting point to help guide them to dive deeper into specific sectors.

It is also aimed for business owners to catch up in this difficult to understand arena and how it could be utilised in their own businesses. Blockchain will be either an opportunity or a threat!

As a business owner I needed guidance and opinion when undertaking changes within my own businesses. When new technology arrives and it's full of extremely intelligent individuals or companies, it helps to be up to speed with all the terminologies and use cases to enable me to navigate around what could be achieved and how it could be delivered without the fuss. I always want to understand how it works in the 'real world' and examples on how it solves problems. There are problems that don't need to be solved! There are so many brilliant applications but sometimes it's too complicated to be successful.

I have written this book that puts context in how we got here and in a manner that anyone can grasp.

My involvement on Blockchain projects is gathering momentum. I have invested in Crypto, downloaded wallets, minted NFTS, started building a website on Blockchain and now acting as an Ambassador for two amazing Blockchain projects. I'm sure this will help with writing my future books which is now also a passion.

FORWARD
BY CLIVE AROSKIN

I met the author fifteen years ago when we were introduced on a telecommunications infrastructure project. Multiple parties were using very clever technology for providing mobile signals to remote areas where no signal was possible. Imagine an aircraft landing in the desert that needed a repair and a team had to get to the location and fix the problem! Well, not having much signal would put the team at a disadvantage! Using some great technology, at that time, we could create a 'communication bubble' to maintain information flow when on-site. We went on to work on multiple projects together, always exploring possibilities of problem solving! Our favourite phrase was, '...blue sky and future'! Solving a problem was the driver and source of excitement for both of us.

I then went on to invest in some Cryptocurrency with friends of mine, unfortunately I sold too early, but, became fascinated with Blockchain technology and Cryptocurrency and the applications that it could serve for the Gaming industry in particular. As with most technologies that are new, they don't always solve the problems very well to begin with. My own journey which is now over four years with my company, as Chief Operating Officer, Gaimin.io, has been, let me say, very full time and has had many bumps in the road to get to where we are today and to listing our own project in the next few months at long last!

So, four years ago I remember discussing the project with the author and unusually, he didn't get it! He liked the idea of Cryptocurrency and a new payment mechanism where international payments could happen in minutes rather than a week, which was always a problem in some of his business projects. Plus, he didn't like all the fees! But, he couldn't get his head around Blockchain!

However, during the last four years he has been a source of enthusiasm and business knowledge and I was able to use him as a sounding board for Gaimin as it progressed through its various stages of growth. And, of course he now 'gets it'! So much so that he has been extremely enthusiastic with the project and now acts as an 'Ambassador' for the company.

When his enthusiasm encouraged him to research for writing a book, I was able to return my knowledge and experience to help him on his journey. We have had many hours of Zoom video calls as the 'Pandemic' hit last year, 2020/21, discussing Blockchain and Cryptocurrency and the future it will have. I am certain there were many other contributors to this book other than myself!

The author wanted to write a book which was easy to read and understand and to provide an overview in simple 'non techie' language. Normally, you would aim a book at a particular type of reader. But, this book was aimed at his friends, those that were interested in Cryptocurrency investing, for his business associates that he has known for many years, that now would like to know more about this technology and how it will affect their existing business models or could potentially enhance their own product offerings. The book provides the reader with a foundation of this new era of technology that is growing at such a speed that it's impossible to ignore. But, also inspires people to what the possibilities are.

I would say 'The Blockchain Future', is 'part one' of your journey and I'm positive that the author's future books will continue to explore the 'niches' that Blockchain technology enables. It will certainly provide you with some conversational ammunition and get you thinking, that's for sure!

COO Gaimin.io Ltd, 55 King Street, Manchester, England

CONTENTS

Acknowledgments 11
Introduction 13

1. Bitcoin Beginnings and the Crypto Rush 19
2. Blockchain and its Basic Structure 35
3. Tokens - The Difference Between Coins and Tokens 51
4. Security and the Blockchain 67
5. Decentralized Applications - what are they and will the experience be the same? 83
6. Buying a piece of art or a football shirt as a digital asset - it might not be that crazy! 97
7. FaceBook getting in on the action! And why that may not be a good thing even though we 'love' Facebook! 113
8. A New Blockchain-Based Infrastructure for Social Media 129
9. Mobile Phones and Blockchain 145
10. The Internet and Web 3.0 - the New Decentralized Internet for Everyone - it's Already Here 159

Conclusion 175

ACKNOWLEDGMENTS

For my daughter Lily. This is why I do it.

For all those who helped me on this journey and every other journey before that! You know who you are.

87 common words and terminologies to help you along your Blockchain and Crypto journey.

Just scan the QR Code and download!

INTRODUCTION

Over recent years, cryptocurrency has generated more headlines than any other phenomenon in the world of finance. It has achieved things that no other investment mechanism has ever achieved, in a timescale that is barely believable. And it has resonated with a new generation of Internet-savvy entrepreneurs and consumers, who almost intrinsically understand its particular qualities and advantages.

Yet as important as cryptocurrency has been in liberalizing finance and currency, the most important revolution in this sphere is still to occur. This is due to technology that has always underpinned cryptocurrency, without ever attracting the frenzied attention associated with the express escalation in the value of Bitcoin.

The blockchain is the technology that makes cryptocurrency possible. It is an incredible innovation that makes it possible to compile huge registers of transactions, which can not only be updated in real-time, but also retain the privacy of those transactions indefinitely. The blockchain guarantees equality, granting all participants within a system equal access, while also ensuring that the vandalism of the system underlying the blockchain is impossible.

This is no mean feat. It is something that has only become conceivable due to the paradigm shift that has occurred via what is sometimes described as the Technological Age. This whirlwind has swept up each and every one of us, at least in the Western world, in recent years. The unstoppable force created by technology can be exciting; offering a wealth of new opportunities and experiences. And it can be inspirational; enticing us with the possibility of exploring new frontiers and solving epoch-defining problems.

But, perhaps above all else, it can be difficult to understand and keep up! The world revolves at a lightning pace nowadays, and the breakneck speed of change means that grasping the latest zeitgeist can be challenging. Technological development has been a fundamental part of human society since the first industrial revolution, but this change has certainly accelerated in the 21st century.

Cryptocurrency is a succinct illustrator of this trend, as it has become almost mainstream in its scope, yet remains misunderstood by many. The mainstream media has played a rather dismal role in this process, doing little to foster comprehension. But the fact remains that many people don't really understand why cryptocurrency exists, can't envisage why an alternative form of currency is required, and certainly couldn't offer an accurate explanation of the underpinning blockchain technology.

This is a distinctive aspect of cryptocurrency. There have always been new inventions, new technologies, new innovations in our lives. But, previously, we understood what they were used for! It was clear that the video recorder was used for...recording TV! And the value of this was immediately evident. When motorised cars first arrived they must have sent shockwaves around the world, but, over time, it was obvious that they delivered immediate convenience.

Even an invention as relatively complex as the personal computer wasn't completely befuddling. It actually took much longer for computers to become a fixture in people's homes than the pioneers initially asserted. On YouTube, you can watch an interview with Steve Jobs in 1981, where he asserts that Apple's mission is to make personal computing part of everyday life, and that although he had yet to achieve this, he hoped it would be the case within five years. In reality, home computing for anything other than gaming had made virtually no market penetration at all in 1986! It was only the advent of the Internet that made computers 'must have' items for every home.

And indeed it is the Internet that has enabled the crypto revolution. The pace of adoption and growth in cryptocurrency has been staggering. Yet most people have yet to embrace cryptocurrency on any level, and there is also arguably something of a generational gulf. It certainly seems that crypto appeal to millennials much more than older people - a Piplsay study in May 2021 found that half of millennials own cryptocurrency; a much higher percentage than any other surveyed demographic.

Not only do many people not understand the blockchain, cryptocurrency, NFTs, and a host of related topics, they also don't see their potential. Cryptocurrency is still often viewed as a novelty, a gimmick, a fly-by-night obscurity that couldn't possibly exist alongside the good old dollar. However, increasingly, that view isn't shared by the mainstream financial industry. Institutional and investment money is rapidly flowing into cryptocurrency. While banks and other major financial institutions may initially have been hostile towards cryptos, their attitude now ranges from a tacit acceptance of the concept to outright enthusiasm.

And the innovation of the blockchain is even more important, delivering myriad possibilities and advancements that will help shape an entirely new human culture. It is therefore critical to understand the technology underpinning this invention, as blockchain represents a massive opportunity, and one where it's still possible to get in on the ground floor.

So the aim of this book is to demystify this incredible contemporary phenomenon that seems to be both simultaneously infamous and unfathomable! Within these pages, we will walk you through everything that is latest and greatest about cryptocurrency and blockchain technology, and unveil the direction that the niche is headed.

Cryptocurrency may already be one of the most exciting, disruptive, controversial and spectacularly successful innovations in the entire history of finance. But this is just the beginning.

CHAPTER 1
BITCOIN BEGINNINGS AND THE CRYPTO RUSH

IN 2008, the reputation and stability of the banking industry had plummeted to an unprecedented low.

The specifics of this have been tremendously well-documented. But one of the most compelling symbols came on 9th October, 2008, when the digital clock in New York that documents the national debt in the United States ran out of digits. The total admitted government debt had exceeded $10 trillion. This was seen as a symbol of unchecked capitalism run amok, of the authorities fundamentally failing, while still claiming that we should trust them as they have our best interests at heart!

Of course, the situation certainly hasn't improved since then. At the time of writing, the national debt of the

United States has nearly tripled to $29 trillion! No doubt it will be over $30 trillion by the time that you read this!

As economic carnage that will never be forgotten tore across the planet, the situation was eerily similar in other Western nations. For example, at the time the UK national debt was over £900 billion (now £2.5 trillion!), while the budget deficit (the amount that the country is overspending in budgetary terms annually) was £163 billion in 2011.[1] In May, 2010, *The Guardian* reported that Britain had the largest deficit among European Union countries, although many other countries also had massive budget deficits.

Nations are in debt, banks are in debt, people are in debt. It seems quite reasonable to pose the old Ciceronian adage - cui bono? Who benefits? The answer is that there is a whole tranche of investment and central banks that benefit hugely from the situation.

DERIVATIVES CASINO

Throughout the early years of the 21st century, banks were treating the financial system as a casino, merrily gambolling and gambling away with trillions of dollars worth of debt. Many people do not realize that financial instruments have been created which enable banks to trade debt. There seems to be little justification for this, other than sheer, cynical greed.

One such example of this is Credit Default Swaps (CDS). These are a form of derivative, which essentially provide major financial institutions and traders with the opportunity to make bets on debt. A CDS is literally an agreement that the seller of the contract will compensate the buyer in the event of a debt default. But, in reality, they are often owned by parties who have no direct insurable interest in the loan; referred to as 'naked' CDS.

The practices associated with CDS and other derivatives contracts have been widely cited as being instrumental in the global financial crisis. But this isn't some insight from hindsight; the alarm bells were ringing loud and clear ahead of the crisis itself. As early as 2008, Money Morning reported that CDS were the real reason for the financial problems that the world was experiencing, and a week later, Newsweek opined that CDS was a "monster that ate Wall Street", and likened the creation of the CDS as being equivalent to the creation of the atomic bomb.[2]

This was not an overreaction, while Newsweek certainly wasn't the only publication offering this viewpoint. In 2010, Market Oracle stated that "Credit Default Swaps threaten the whole system", having previously described CDS as "Weapons of Mass Financial Destruction".[3] This was far from temperate language, at a time when the value of the CDS market was $62 trillion. By comparison, in 2009, the GDP of the United States was just over $14 trillion.

CBS News commented that CDS "could seriously threaten the world's markets", Daily Markets described the situation as a "horrific derivatives bubble that threatens to destroy not only the U.S. economy but the entire world financial system", and Silicon Valley Watcher pointed out that "when derivatives unravel significantly the entire world economy would be at peril. The derivatives market collapse could make the housing and stock market collapses look incidental".[4]

At the time, the major players in the financial sector would no doubt have defended their CDS conduct to the death, and belittled anyone that suggested that it was anything other than virtuous, admirable and a critical growth engine for the economy. Conversely, after the system virtually collapsed, the European Parliament banned naked Credit Default Swaps.[5]

SYSTEM PROBLEMS

In short, by the time that the global financial crisis hit, around the period 2008-10, it wasn't difficult to predict that the system could experience problems. In fact, anyone in the know had already anticipated it. When it occurred, the consequences for people across the world were severe, most memorably encapsulated by the policy of austerity that was widely implemented. The governments and the banks created the problems – the people paid the price.

Meanwhile, the banking sector escaped virtually any consequences for its actions whatsoever, receiving a torrent of public money to assuage any difficulties that they may have experienced. There was a two-tier attitude towards the 'haves' and 'have nots', and it seemed inevitable that there would be some blowback.

Eventually rioting in Europe became widespread, partly resulting from proposals to slash public expenditure, services and a raft of new taxation laws. Amongst the plans of the Greek government, was a policy of banning early retirement, with the compliant UK *Times* newspaper happily describing the previous Greek pension scheme for public sector workers as "generous". The Greek public sector worker would now be required to work until the age of 63, although this figure has already been pushed back to 67.[6]

In March, 2009, the *Daily Telegraph* gleefully reported that the time had come to "retire retirement", in an article subtitled, "in the long term, the only answer is to abandon compulsory retirement". In July 2010, the BBC dutifully reported that the government was planning to scrap the fixed retirement age, and in January 2011, these plans were finalized and formally announced.[7] In May, 2011, the *Daily Telegraph* reported that "employees in their twenties, thirties and forties could find themselves working beyond their 75th or even 80th birthday".[8]

In 2007, HBOS announced profits of £5.7 billion, and claimed that this eye-watering figure "helps drive the economy".[9] Just ten months later, the banking group was one of the recipients of £37 billion of public money, due to apparent gaping holes in its balance sheet[10].

In short, people of modest means were having state support swept from under them, while multi-billion dollar institutions, who had behaved phenomenally irresponsibly, were bailed out with the tax money of everyday citizens.

No wonder people felt slightly cheated.

It was in the context of this extraordinary and regrettable period of socio-economic history that the birth of cryptocurrencies must be placed. Bitcoin didn't just emerge from a period of mild dissatisfaction, it was created at a time when some of the most iconic cities in Europe were ablaze with rioting. And this was not rioting aimed at one specific policy, it was not single-issue activism, the subject of this rioting was crystal clear. The system has deceived and defrauded us! We want change!

It is not an overstatement to describe the concept of cryptocurrency as a revolution. Throughout recent human history, currency has been centrally issued, controlled by an omnipotent authority, and distributed among the people via economic activity. Generally speaking, most people accept this, and economists will go to arcane lengths to defend this, deeming it to be as natural and inevitable as the sun rising in the morning.

Of course, this is total nonsense. There is no inherent reason why modes of payment and settlement should be centrally controlled. In fact, this is enshrined, for example, in UK law. The Royal Mint notes:

"Legal tender has a very narrow and technical meaning in the settlement of debts. It means that a debtor cannot successfully be sued for non-payment if he pays into court in legal tender. It does not mean that any ordinary transaction has to take place in legal tender or only within the amount denominated by the legislation. Both parties are free to agree to accept any form of payment (note: my emphasis) whether legal tender or otherwise according to their wishes."[11]

MONEY AND FAITH

Sterling, the dollar, the euro, in fact any modern currency that you can name, are examples of fiat currency, fiat from the Latin meaning "let it be made". Keynes defined fiat currency as, "state-issued money which is neither legally convertible to any other thing, nor fixed in value in terms of any objective standard". Investopedia defines fiat money as, "currency that a government declared to be legal tender, even though it has no intrinsic value, and is not backed by reserves. Historically, most currencies were based on physical commodities, such as gold or silver, but fiat money is based solely on faith", and goes on to say, "most of the world's paper money is fiat money. Because fiat money is not linked to physical reserves, it risks becoming worthless due to hyperinflation. If people lose faith in a nation's paper currency, the money will no longer hold any value".

Money does not have any intrinsic value, nor is it legally required to exist. You can make a payment with anything, if the other party is in agreement. And the value of money is based on faith; that is indeed what 'fiat currency' means. That's potentially fine in times where people are willing to invest faith in the authorities, but when that trust is compromised or shattered entirely, the system of central control no longer serves any legitimate purpose.

It is important to understand all of this before considering the birth of cryptocurrency. Bitcoin wasn't dreamt up in a dark room amid an acid trip. It didn't appear entirely by accident, or due to some unfounded malcontent. It was a direct consequence of the virtual collapse of the global financial system, and the total collapse of many people's faith in the authorities and financial sector.

Bitcoin was born out of the firmly believed notion that the central authorities had too much control. It was a product of the fractured relationship between governments, banks and the general population, as well as a libertarian tendency to seek alternatives to centralized control.

Nonetheless, Bitcoin may have been a pioneer, but it wasn't the first example of digitalized currency. Several digital cash technologies preceded the concept of cryptocurrency, so it wasn't the outlandish idea that it was often branded some years ago. In fact, the notion of solutions to computational puzzles having value dates back to 1992, proposed at that time by cryptographers Cynthia Dwork and Moni Naor.[12]

However, Bitcoin was the first expression of the transformative idea of alternative currency as a societally beneficial platform. From the initialisation of Bitcoin as a concept, its still anonymous creators believed that cryptocurrencies had huge potential, and that Bitcoin was, in fact, required from a moral and ethical perspective.

THE FINANCIAL COUNTERCULTURE

While the identity of Bitcoin's creator, Satoshi Nakamoto, remains a mystery, the ethos of his cryptocurrency creation was clear from day one. The system was intended to drive a financial counterculture, to provide a liberating and decentralized alternative to currencies, banks and financial systems that had overreached their purpose.

During its early days, Bitcoin gathered momentum from a community of interested parties and investors, who believed in the potential and essence of the project. It was only from the enthusiasm and investment of faith in the project that Bitcoin was even able to get off the ground; in this sense, the founders had already proved that it was a viable alternative to money, and that anything could become currency if enough people simply believed in it enough.

Cryptocurrency was a concept that resonated with young people in particular, and it's no coincidence that members of the millennial generation have been the most enthusiastic investors in the project. It has been widely documented that people in the 18-30 demographic have been more severely impacted by the general climate of financial malaise than any other. They were ready for the alternative, for a system of currency that was controlled by the people, rather than a central authority, and Bitcoin provided it.

Aside from its libertarian outlook, Bitcoin also offered clear advantages over facets of the existing system. One of the most prominent is that peer-to-peer money makes it possible to send currency to a third party without incurring expense, or at least with considerably smaller fees that are associated with traditional services, such as Western Union, Moneygram or banks. This was just one way that Bitcoin threatened to overturn a monopoly, and put the power of payment back in the hands of the people.

MINING ETHOS

There could be no bigger symbol of this decentralized accessibility than the fact that Bitcoin is 'mined', and can be acquired by anyone. Contrast this with traditional fiat currencies, which can only be printed by a central authority, whose issuance is carefully controlled, and in relation to which people will be sent to jail for even attempting to print their own.

The creators of Bitcoin attempted to tap into the existing mindset and beliefs of goldbugs and others who were sceptical about fiat currency from day one, aligning the token with commodities and both practically and figuratively associating Bitcoin with the gold standard. This principle that some measure should control the amount of currency in circulation had long since been removed by the financial system by the time that Bitcoin emerged, but many people believed this to be a grotesque mistake. Bitcoin would only allow 21 million tokens into existence, thus mirroring the finite qualities of the gold standard, and attracting many new believers to its exciting new platform.

When Bitcoin first launched, there was little apparent reason for most people to pay attention, and certainly not the big boys of the financial sector. They fully believed themselves to be untouchable. As Matt Taibbi noted in an article in *Rolling Stone* at the height of the financial crisis: "If the Justice Department fails to give the American people a chance to judge [the financial crisis in court] it will confirm once and for all the embarrassing truth: that the law in America is subjective, and crime is defined not by what you did, but by who you are".[13]

Needless to say, no such action was forthcoming. Instead, governments all over the world entered into a massive program of quantitative easing, essentially money printing, which was widely considered to be a monumental failure in its goals. By this time, Bitcoin had grown from a non-entity in the eyes of the world's top banks, to a growing platform that was beginning to create a buzz regarding its utilization and value. The heady climbs in price that were to follow had yet to really begin, but the token had escalated to a value of $88 by March 2013;[14] an increase of 220,000% from the mere 4 cents that each token could be sold for in 2010.

RUNNING SCARED

As Bitcoin began to make headline news, the banker-class increasingly reacted against it. There have been many wild haymakers swung by the financial aristocracy since Bitcoin became a contender, but two of the most infamous have come from Bank of America and JP Morgan. Analysts at Bank of America decried Bitcoin as "volatile" and "impractical", while the CEO of JP Morgan, Jamie Dimon, slammed the concept as "stupid" and a "fraud". Later, the investment bank created a cryptocurrency to help settle payments between clients in its wholesale payments business.

Governments were also sceptical about the Bitcoin revolution, at least initially. The crypto token clearly represented a challenge to the existing order, and the establishment responded as could be expected; they closed ranks. There was a frosty response to Bitcoin and other cryptos as they became headline news, mainly for a very simple reason; this was a form of currency that could never be centrally controlled.

However, over time the position of banks and governments has softened, partly due to sheer necessity. Bitcoin is here to stay, as is the concept of blockchain, and there is nothing that can be done at this stage to stymie the relentless momentum of the cryptocurrency revolution. Instead, a regulatory framework has been created, as both governments and the traditional heavyweights of the financial sector accept that they must coexist with this new financial upstart.

Bitcoin, and for that matter a wealth of other crypto products, ensure that the ultra-secure flow of information is immutable. The blockchain cannot be controlled by big banks, big tech, or even big governments. And while currency and investment have been the primary use cases for the blockchain, this certainly isn't the end of the story. Anyone can now create new ways of doing things much more quickly, and retain the right to create an entirely new ecosystem, which can then become open-source and community-driven.

Blockchain is now part of a vibrant and growing culture. The only limit to the concept is our collective imagination.

———

On 3rd January 2009, the Bitcoin network came into existence with Satoshi Nakamoto mining the genesis block of the cryptocurrency (block number 0), which had a reward of 50 tokens. Embedded in the coinbase of this block was the text:

The Times...Jan/03/2009...Chancellor on brink of second bailout for banks.

References

1. *UK Parliament.* (2010). The economic recovery and the budget deficit: key issues for the 2010 Parliament.
2. Philips, M. (2008). How Credit Default Swaps Became a Timebomb. *Newsweek.*
3. Dorsch, G. (2008). Credit Default Swaps Weapons of Financial Mass Destruction. *Market Oracle.*
4. Matai, D., K. (2009). The Size of the Derivatives Bubble = $190K Per Person on Planet. *The Center for Research on Globalization.*
5. *EU Business.* (2011). Euro-Parliament bans 'naked' credit default swaps.
6. Becatoros, E. (2017). 'They stole my money': Greek dreams of retirement turn sour. *Ekathimerini.com.*
7. *BBC.* (2011). Compulsory retirement age at 65 fully abolished.
8. Prince, R. (2011). Budget 2011: Younger staff will work to 80 under pension link to rising lifespans. *The Daily Telegraph.*
9. *The Scotsman.* (2007). £5.7bn HBOS profit 'helps drive economy'.
10. Wearden, G. (2008). British government unveils £37bn banking bail-out plan. *The Guardian.*
11. *The Royal Mint.* (2021). What are the legal tender

amounts acceptable for the United Kingdom coins?.
12. Dwork, C. & Naor, M. (1992). Pricing via Processing or Combatting Junk Mail. *Advances in Cryptology '92*, pp 139-147.
13. Taibbi, M. (2011). The People vs. Goldman Sachs. Rolling Stone.
14. Farrell, M. (2013). Bitcoin prices surge post-Cyprus bailout. CNN.

CHAPTER 2
BLOCKCHAIN AND ITS BASIC STRUCTURE

WHILE IT IS cryptocurrencies such as Bitcoin that have made headlines and attracted the attention of investors, the foundation for this revolution lies elsewhere. It is blockchain technology that makes cryptocurrency possible, and which indeed promises a raft of other innovations in the foreseeable future.

But what exactly is the blockchain? This innovation is effectively a public ledger of all transactions associated with a cryptocurrency. But the technology also has a variety of other use cases, which will become more apparent and prominent as more people understand the potential of blockchains.

THE ROOTS OF THE BLOCKCHAIN

Although the rise of cryptocurrency is a relatively recent phenomenon, its roots actually date back several decades. Cryptographer David Chaum first proposed a blockchain-like protocol in his dissertation "Computer Systems Established, Maintained, and Trusted by Mutually Suspicious Groups", way back in 1982.[1] Further important theoretical work was contributed by Stuart Haber and W. Scott Stornetta,[2] so by the time that Bitcoin was first conceptualized in 2008, the foundation of this system was already established theoretically.

Nonetheless, the work of (still anonymous) Bitcoin founder Satoshi Nakamoto in 2008 was undoubtedly the most important step in implementing blockchain technology on a grand scale. Nakamoto designed a method of timestamping blocks that were added to a chain, without requiring them to be signed by a central party. This design was implemented a year later when Bitcoin was produced, and this has proven to be the most revolutionary idea in recent financial history.

This provides some background on the development of the blockchain, but the actual technology can still sometimes confuse people due to its complexity. Well, in fact, the core concept behind the blockchain is rather straightforward - it is simply a type of database. All the blockchain represents is a collection of information stored electronically on a computer system. In cryptocurrencies, these blockchains are then used for a variety of purposes, most notably to ensure that the systems function correctly, and that every single transaction is recorded on a decentralized and public ledger.

BUILDING THE BLOCKCHAIN

The sheer scale of some of the large cryptocurrency projects means that the blockchain needs to be housed on a network of services hosted by powerful computers. This is absolutely critical in order to deliver the computational power and storage capacity that is necessary for many users to access these sometimes vast databases simultaneously. Unfortunately, you couldn't run Bitcoin from one laptop! It does require rather more resources than that!

Where blockchains differ from databases is in the way that data is structured. As the name suggests, blocks are key to the blockchain, as these are a way of collecting information together in groups. Each of these blocks has a certain level of storage capacity, and when the blocks included on the network are filled with data, they are 'chained' onto the previously created block, forming what has become informally known as the blockchain.

The entirety of the blockchain represents all of this information chained together, and the evolution of cryptocurrencies and other innovations that utilize blockchain technology, thus, this record of the transactions is constantly growing and evolving. In this sense, the blockchain is a highly organic technology, which provides a living and breathing record of some of the most complex systems in the world, while making them accessible for people of all levels of technical understanding. Therefore, the blockchain can be much more readily compared to cloud services rather than traditional database systems. Unlike database systems accessed via a conventional computer, the blockchain is almost limitlessly flexible, and is capable of delivering a staggering number of use cases.

So the basic functioning of the blockchain isn't particularly difficult to understand. However, the advantages of the technology aren't always immediately obvious. But that doesn't mean that they don't exist, and indeed they are numerous.

DECENTRALIZED PLATFORM

The first and most obvious principle that underlies both Bitcoin and blockchain technology in general, and indeed virtually the entire niche of cryptocurrency, is the notion that this system should be completely decentralized. Indeed, that was one of the primary motivations of the founder of Bitcoin; as discussed in the previous chapter, it was a direct response to the traditional banking system, which was viewed as authoritarian and too deeply controlled by far too few people.

This can never apply to Bitcoin or other cryptocurrencies based on blockchain technology, as the innovation effectively consists of thousands of computers. Each of these computers, or groups of computers, which collectively comprise the blockchain are located in different geographical spaces, and they are all operated by completely different people. This enables Bitcoin and other cryptocurrencies to deliver a completely decentralized model, meaning that they can never be controlled by one person or group of people. This achievement is undoubtedly one of the crowning glories of Nakamoto, and is central to the liberalizing and revolutionary potential of cryptocurrency.

It's also important to briefly explain that the way the blockchain is structured builds a failsafe element into the system. The Bitcoin blockchain, for example, is widely available to users, and therefore there is always the question of what occurs if someone chooses to tamper with this critical record of transactions. But the reality is that this is impossible, due to the thousands of nodes used by the system.

Each of these nodes includes a full record of the data that has been stored on the blockchain since its inception. This can vary depending on the blockchain project in question, however for Bitcoin in particular, and most cryptocurrencies in general, this data is the entire history of all transactions. If one node has an error, this will then cause thousands of other nodes as a reference point to correct themselves. By using this failsafe mechanism, the history of transactions in each block that comprise the blockchain is completely irresistible, as all other nodes will cross-reference one another, easily pinpointing the maladapted node.

This also enables the blockchain to be particularly transparent, with all transactions available to all users, or indeed anyone who chooses to become a user in the future. This is often contrasted with the somewhat secretive world of traditional banking. Yet despite the transparency of Bitcoin, the safeguards that have been built into the system mean that transparency can be delivered without any risk to the overall architecture of the currency.

MINING CRYPTOS

These aspects of the blockchain are all fascinating and valuable, but beginners to the space often wonder how coins are indeed created. Again, there is a massive contrast here between the existing financial system and cryptocurrencies. Everyone reading this book will realize that they have absolutely no right to create currency, unless they happen to be the Governor of the Bank of England, Chair of the Board of Governors of the

Federal Reserve System, or President of the European Central Bank! If Jerome Powell, Andrew Bailey or Christine Lagarde are reading this, may I offer my most sincere apologies!

Nonetheless, most of us don't have the right to create currency! In fact, attempting to do so is a very serious criminal offence. Money comes into existence based on a combination of government policy and central bank issuance, although increasingly government policy has been divorced from this process. It is not for no reason that many people assume that central banks literally control the world.

Conversely, the creation of units with Bitcoin is available to anyone. This is achieved via mining, which is the process by which new Bitcoin tokens enter into circulation. This process also plays a role in the maintenance and development of the blockchain ledger. The actual process of mining depends on the cryptocurrency in question, but in the case of Bitcoin, it requires sophisticated computers to solve extremely complicated computational problems. When these problems are solved correctly, a miner is rewarded with a token.

It should also be noted that the total number of Bitcoin tokens is capped at 21 million; creating a finite supply (other cryptos also have similar measures in place). This is then another area in which the system has been contrasted with that of fiat currencies, which theoretically have absolutely no limits placed on the amount of money in circulation. Indeed, it is indisputable that all fiat currencies have steadily declined in value over time, and this is even acknowledged by the authorities, which continually track the so-called rate of inflation (although they do it in the most misleading and inaccurate way possible!).

VOTING AND DEMOCRACY

Another democratic aspect of Bitcoin and other cryptocurrencies when it comes to mining is that successfully acquiring tokens can provide you with voting power when changes are proposed in the protocol of the system. This aspect is significant, as several cryptocurrency projects have been 'forked' - effectively split into one or more new tokens - and the fact that the Bitcoin community has a degree of influence on the decision-making process related to the currency was an entirely new concept when it first emerged.

This is akin to the active central bank in your country knocking on your front door and asking your opinion on interest rates; needless to say, I wouldn't recommend holding your breath for that to happen! It is perhaps this aspect of cryptocurrency above all else that has led to hostility from the traditional financial aristocracy, as they simply don't believe that 'the great unwashed' should have any say in the financial system. In many ways, Bitcoin and other cryptocurrencies are a wake-up bomb to the general population, if they can only understand the importance of the concept. Why should they spend their entire lives having an unelected and unaccountable bureaucracy of elitists ruling their lives via the mechanism of currency? While the people never get any say in the process whatsoever?

Of course, the mainstream media and the authorities themselves continually perpetuate the impression that those who run the system are highly respectable and responsible, and motivated only by doing the best for the general population. We could be completely credulous and accept that at face value, or we could instead look at the recent and oft-quoted words of Karl Schwab, the Founder and Executive Chairman of the World Economic Forum, who has already decided that we will "own nothing and be happy about it". Again, the mainstream media would have us believe that we have misinterpreted these comments, and that the World Economic Forum sincerely wishes to "harness the innovations of the Fourth Industrial Revolution to support the public good."[3] I'll leave the reader to be the judge of that.

So Bitcoin and cryptocurrencies are a direct response to this culture of elitism. They are a solution that spans continents, so they can be accessed by anyone and everyone, all over the planet, with all people having equal access and rights. There is no restriction of trade and development associated with cryptocurrencies, while the technology also makes cross-border payments both more convenient and considerably more affordable. Some crypto projects, including Ripple, have indeed focused on this quality, offering it as a particularly viable use case.

SHUTTING DOWN

Furthermore, the nature of the blockchain ensures that it's completely impossible for Bitcoin, or other similar tokens, to be shut down. This was confirmed recently by the chief executive of the world's biggest cryptocurrency exchange, Binance CEO Changpeng Zhao, who commented that he didn't "think anyone can shut [Bitcoin] down now, given that this technology, this concept, is in 500 million people's heads. You can't erase that."[4] Zhao compared the likelihood of shutting down Bitcoin and other cryptocurrencies to refusing to accept Amazon and other dot-coms business models, which have unquestionably reshaped commerce.

Another important aspect of the blockchain, which adds value to Bitcoin and other cryptocurrencies, is the fact that data privacy isn't solely in the hands of a profit-oriented board of directors. Again, it comes back to a simple and central point; no one entity can control what is seen on the Bitcoin blockchain, nor how its community engages with the token. The rise of Bitcoin hasn't come about due to any centralized initiative, it has simply occurred due to mass participation in the system from millions of people all over the globe. It is only from their belief in Bitcoin that it has risen to its position of prominence, but now tens of millions of people understand the value of the cryptocurrency and blockchain concept.

While the blockchain is intrinsically associated with cryptocurrency, it doesn't mean by any stretch of the imagination that the concept is limited to currency systems. In the long run, the blockchain provides an ideal technology for multiple systems and industries, one that can revolutionize and improve many areas of life, just as has already been achieved with currency and payment systems.

It is the immutable nature of the blockchain that is so valuable, as it provides a permanent record that goes way beyond any traditional systems in this area, which can never be tampered with. Transactions are fast and transparent, the system is self-sustaining, no intermediary fees are required, and constant improvements can be made.

OTHER INDUSTRIES

While the blockchain concept has yet to become widely implemented in mainstream industry, there have been examples of some major companies adopting the innovation in their everyday practices. For example, Unilever, the huge consumer goods company that owns brands such as Ben & Jerry's, Dove, Vaseline and Knorr, is already utilizing blockchain technology as part of its efforts to tackle deforestation. The company previously integrated blockchain technology to restructure the way demographic and location data are collected, saved, and verified.[5]

Elsewhere, Walmart is already actively using blockchain technology as a critical element of its supply ecosystem. Walmart tested its Hyperledger Fabric blockchain-based food traceability system with mangoes in the United States, and found the time needed to trace their provenance rapidly diminished from 7 days to...2.2 seconds! [6] And the credit card company Visa has also found a valuable use for technology based on blockchain architecture. Visa B2B Connect has used tapped into the borderless quality of the blockchain in its international payment system.[7]

This is just the tip of the iceberg when it comes to implementing blockchain in industrial settings. The technology is set to have a disruptive impact across multiple industries, with banking, cybersecurity, supply chain management, healthcare and government services set to be the biggest beneficiaries.

In banking, the blockchain will eliminate the need for a middleman, driving down fees, while also providing exceptional security. The blockchain will help cybersecurity firms more rapidly identify threats. The technology can play a major role in supply chain management, facilitating traceability across the entire supply chain. Blockchain also removes central authorities, which can be extremely helpful in healthcare settings.

The concept can help healthcare providers enhance privacy, security, and medical records, while also shoring private data up against cyber-attacks. United Healthcare is one such provider that is already utilizing blockchain technology in its operation.[8] And another area where blockchain technology could come in particularly useful is during elections. The whole system is designed to make voting reliable, transparent and anonymous; thus, blockchain-based electoral solutions such as MiVote have already emerged.[9]

As the value of the blockchain becomes more apparent, we can expect to see many more companies and industries embracing this revolutionary concept. The sky is the limit for a technology that only really emerged just over a decade ago. And this will become increasingly apparent as blockchain increasingly seeps into the public consciousness. The concept has already achieved a lot, without many people being aware of what the blockchain represents, let alone its potential.

But the expansion of the technology is already apparent. In August 2014, the bitcoin blockchain file size, containing records of all transactions that have occurred on the network, reached 20GB. At the time of writing, it has now expanded 18-fold from this point, to approximately 360GB. This is testimony to the number of people that already recognize the value of the blockchain, and the scale of participants in the existing infrastructure.

The blockchain may be a huge part of our collective future. But the future is already here.

References

1. Lee, D. (1982). Computer Systems Established, Maintained and Trusted by Mutually Suspicious Group. *University of California.*
2. Haber, S. & Stornetta, W., Scott. (1991). How to time-stamp a digital document. *Journal of Cryptology volume 3, pp. 99–111.*
3. Schwab, K. (2020). Now is the time for a 'great reset' . *World Economic Forum.*
4. Shen, N. (2021). No One Can Shut Down Bitcoin, Says Binance CEO CZ. *Coindesk.*

5. Tran, S. (2020). Unilever to Use Blockchain for Transparency and Traceability to Achieve Deforestation-Free Supply Chain by 2023. *Blockchain News*.
6. *Hyperledger*. (2021). Case Study: How Walmart brought unprecedented transparency to the food supply chain with Hyperledger Fabric.
7. *Visa*. (2021). Transforming B2B Payments for the Digital Age.
8. *United Health Group*. (2021). The Future of Digital Health Care.
9. Karp, P. (2017). MiVote aims to shake up democratic process with a click and a tap. *The Guardian*.

CHAPTER 3
TOKENS - THE DIFFERENCE BETWEEN COINS AND TOKENS

IN THE WORLD OF CRYPTOCURRENCY, the terms 'coins' and 'tokens' are frequently used interchangeably. This is perfectly natural, but it is also technically incorrect. Another term that can be bracketed with coins and tokens is 'digital assets', and it's therefore important to understand the difference between these three different aspects of cryptocurrency.

As we discussed in previous chapters, cryptocurrencies are decentralized systems that are built on blockchain or distributed ledger technology. This makes it possible for a community to enforce the rules associated with the system in a transparent fashion. Each of these three terms is related to the blockchain and cryptocurrency, but they have subtly different purposes and definitions.

CRYPTO COINS

Coins are essentially units of exchange that are associated with blockchain networks. While there is no obligation for blockchains to be associated with currency, it is certainly the case currently that most existing blockchains have their own personal coins. These can then be used for payment, as they are effectively digital money. By far the most notable example of coins in this sphere is Bitcoin, although there are many others.

Cryptocurrency coins share many characteristics with traditional fiat currency. They are easily distributed, widely accepted for payment, portable and durable. Where they differ with traditional currencies is in the limited supply available, which is one of the defining characteristics of the cryptocurrency niche.

Bitcoin has a maximum supply of 21 million coins, which is intended to protect against inflation. It is precisely this inflation that is an inbuilt characteristic of the monetary system, due to the inevitable degradation of monetary value caused by the increasing supply of credit. Essentially, when elderly people make misty-eyed comments about some decades ago having been able to catch the train, enjoy a cheeseburger and fries, watch a movie, ride home and still have change from a quarter or tuppence, this is a manifestation of inflation. This is not some inbuilt law of nature, such as the sun rising in the morning, or the tide rushing to shore. It is not inevitable. It is absolutely a function of the monetary system, in which the supply of money continues to expand due to monetary policy, and indeed the fact that there are no such limits placed on the amount of currency and debt in circulation.

FUNGIBILITY

Another important aspect of cryptocurrency coins relates to a word that you will frequently encounter in this field, but which can be a little baffling to the uninitiated. Cryptocurrency coins are fungible. This simply means that crypto coins can be easily exchanged for something of equal value. There is such a thing as non-fungible tokens, and we will discuss this further as the book develops.

In the world of cryptocurrency, coins are inevitably related to the public and open blockchain. This means that all community participants are invited to join in the network and acquire the coins. Cryptocurrency coins can also be sent and received, and in the majority of cases they can be acquired by mining or another similar process, although this doesn't apply to all cryptocurrency projects. As the supply of cryptocurrency coins is also usually finite, there is also a theoretical point at the future when it will no longer be possible to mine the coins.

CRYPTO TOKENS

Conversely, tokens, also frequently referred to as crypto tokens, are units of value that are built on top of existing blockchain networks by the developers and organizations associated with the projects. There are often links and compatibility overlaps between tokens and coins on cryptocurrency networks, but they should be viewed as an entirely different digital asset class.

Cryptocurrency tokens are created by the platforms that are constructed on top of the blockchain network. For example, the native token associated with the hugely influential Ethereum blockchain is ether. But there are many other different tokens that can also be built on the same blockchain, particularly as the structure of Ethereum has become hugely influential and admired. The tokens can then serve a range of purposes on the blockchain, as is reflected among the many great cryptocurrency projects that have been developed. Many blockchains are associated with currency, but there are other possibilities with blockchain as well, with content creation becoming one of the most popular areas.

It's also important to know that there are many different standards used for cryptocurrency tokens. ERC-20 has become the most popular, as it is operable within the Ethereum ecosystem. At the time of writing, Ethereum looks extremely well-placed to establish itself as the most widely used of all blockchains, even including Bitcoin, but the crypto space continues to evolve rapidly, and this is by no means inevitable.

ERC-20 isn't the only standard available. There are also thousands of ERC-721 tokens in circulation, and it is believed that many other standards and token platforms will become popular in the foreseeable future.

SMART CONTRACTS AND PROGRAMMABLE TOKENS

Cryptocurrency tokens are strongly related to smart contracts, which are involved in defining the features and functions of the token in question, as well as several parameters associated with the network. Smart contracts are extremely important in cryptocurrency, and have an almost inherent relationship with tokens. Any successful cryptocurrency token should be programmable, permission-less, free from trust issues, and completely transparent. These are fundamental qualities associated with cryptocurrency projects and tokens, and must be delivered if a platform is to meet the approval of the discerning cryptocurrency community.

Another critical aspect of cryptocurrency tokens is that they tend to be programmable. This means that they can be run on software protocols, which are composed of smart contracts that outline the features and functions of the token, as well as rules of engagement associated with the network. This programmable quality means that tokens are extremely flexible, and that they can be potentially used for multiple purposes. Tokens are also accessible for anyone participating in the system, without any special credentials being required, while roles associated with the protocol should be viewable and verifiable by all participants.

Cryptocurrency tokens can represent virtually anything. Already, there are tokens available that are associated with physical assets, digital assets, real estate, art, processing power, digital storage, and even abstract concepts! In short, if something has value, it can be represented in a cryptocurrency token. It could be a painting, it could be currency, it could be a powerful computer server, it could even theoretically be a sportsman or woman! There is no limit to the utility of crypto tokens, which is what makes them such an exciting concept.

This is where the term 'digital assets' comes in. Cryptocurrency tokens capture a digital asset. As the niche continues to mature, it is expected that these digital assets will only continue to expand and evolve. As more people understand how cryptocurrency operates, the number of use cases and community requirements will expand, and this will only lead to more flexibility and diversity in the cryptocurrency space. This will inevitably be exacerbated by the simple fact that cryptocurrency and the blockchain is almost infinitely less restrictive than any traditional currency platform, as the digital world is based on intangibles. Cryptos can become anything to anyone, and everything to all people. This opens up an array of new social and economic possibilities, which is one of the most compelling arguments for the blockchain.

TYPES OF TOKEN

Another distinction that needs to be briefly covered is the difference between security tokens, equity tokens and utility tokens (there are also payment tokens, but these do not differ significantly from coins). The majority of cryptocurrency tokens are security tokens, particularly for those platforms that ran initial client offerings (ICO). These tokens derive their name from the fact that they are a form of security; a type of financial investment. In this respect, cryptocurrency security tokens are treated similarly to traditional securities.

By contrast, equity tokens offer a stock or share in the company that issues the token. These are pretty rare by comparison, as they make the ICO process considerably more complicated. Finally, utility tokens are also sometimes referred to as application tokens, and provide access to products or services. In this regard, tokens can have completely different purposes, contributing to the diversity of the concept.

There can be confusion over whether a token fits into a particular criterion, but there is legal precedent that provides a guide. In 1946, the Securities and Exchange Commission engaged in a landmark case with W. J. Howey Co.,[1] which is now considered the benchmark for deciding whether transactions should be considered investment contracts or securities. This therefore has an impact on cryptocurrency tokens as well.

If a cryptocurrency token is to be considered a security, it must be derived from an investment of fiat currency, it must support a common enterprise, and investment must be made with an expectation of future profit. This last characteristic in particular does not necessarily apply to all tokens, as some can have more practical purposes.

TOKENS AND DAPPS

Another important aspect of tokens is that most are designed to be used with decentralized applications (dApps). These are apps for programs that run on a blockchain network, rather than utilizing a single computer network. By utilizing this approach, dApps operate outside the control of a single or central authority, meaning that they are more democratized and evolve as part of community activity. There are many examples of tokens that serve some function related to dApps; for example, Musicoin enables users to gain access to music and streaming via the Musicoin platform. And the Binance token reduces fees on the Binance platform by 50%. This is another aspect of tokens which is fundamentally different from coins, as the latter are merely instruments of exchange.

BLOCKCHAIN BUSINESS MODELS

The business and use cases associated with tokens are almost limitless. Another example of an interesting development is WePower, which makes it possible for users to buy and sell electricity on the blockchain via smart contracts. The WePower token literally represents a certain amount of energy, which can fluctuate based on training.

Because the blockchain is extremely flexible and completely decentralized, the technology delivers a wider range of potential business models than have existed previously. The blockchain makes it possible for all businesses to shift their entire operation into a decentralized platform, altering the way that users interact with the system and the way that transactions are conducted.

The fact that this can all be stored inside the blockchain, and never tampered with, is a huge advantage of the innovation. This obviously offers security advantages, but it also means that companies can leverage the transparency of the blockchain to improve the way that their supply chains work. Blockchains are also frequently combined with artificial intelligence and machine learning, creating smart and organic platforms that can achieve tasks in completely different ways than were envisaged previously, as well as offering increased flexibility.

One of the most compelling business models associated with the blockchain is the utility token. Ripple and Stellar are great examples of this model, in which their tokens drive the functionality of the business. Both Ripple and Stellar have become closely affiliated with banks and financial institutions, who can then arrange for fund transfers via the use of the XRP or XLM tokens. This is faster and considerably more cost-effective than any other previously accessible form of transfer, which is now being widely recognized by mainstream financial entities. Hence why Ripple is often advocated to be an ideal cross-border payment system.

BLOCKCHAIN-AS-A-SERVICE

The Blockchain-as-a-Service (BaaS) model makes it possible for businesses to outsource some of their more onerous backend operations, ensuring that they can focus on their shop-floor business. BaaS providers tend to offer services such as user authentication, database management, remote updating, push notifications, cloud storage, and hosting. These can be handled more efficiently than with any form of existing technology. Google Firebase and Microsoft Azure are compelling examples of this approach.

By employing the blockchain in this way, the technology effectively manages and solves all infrastructure and maintenance issues, enabling companies to instead focus on improving their core website functionality, instead of constantly tweaking glitches and bugs. Services such as bandwidth management, optimized allocation of resources, hosting requirements, and enhanced security features are inherent in this approach.

DEVELOPMENT PLATFORMS

Another use case associated with the blockchain is development platforms. These can often be solutions developed by start-ups, which find unique ways to solve existing problems. There are a multitude of advantages of utilizing the blockchain in order to achieve this outcome. Security can be improved, all immutability is removed via higher cryptographic hash functions, and systems become much easier to monitor, trace and audit as a result.

By creating development platforms via the blockchain, trust with the end user is also increased via the transparency of the system. This can provide huge advantages for businesses, and is considered to be one of the growth areas for blockchain technology. Indeed, the CEO of Binance commented that "for our industry to grow we need more entrepreneurs to build real projects."[2] Ethereum founder Vitalik Buterin and Tron founder Justin Sun have also been among the prominent voices encouraging entrepreneurs to build applications that run on other platforms.[3]

It is probably in dApps that blockchain solutions have the most potential for growth. There are so many potential applications that could be delivered by blockchain technology, which would improve the quality of service offered. This process is already happening, and many big businesses are on-board, but the exploration of the blockchain in this area remains in an embryonic state. There is considerable room for development and expansion, particularly as more people become aware of the huge potential of this innovative technology.

TOKENOMICS

One final concept that is important to understand in this area is 'tokenomics'. This refers to a mixture of marketing and pure maths, which enables those implementing blockchain technology to understand the supply and demand characteristics of both the blockchain and cryptocurrency. It sounds a little complex to begin with, but in principle is rather straightforward.

Tokenomics are essentially factors that should be taken into consideration when attempting to predict the underlying value of a certain cryptocurrency project. With traditional currencies, this is achieved via the monitoring of monetary supply and financial data. As mentioned previously, the nature of existing monetary systems mean that they inevitably degrade in value over a period of time.

This doesn't inherently apply to cryptocurrencies, which are often based on fixed supply, although this is not applicable to all coins. For example, the high-profile Dogecoin features issuance guidance that will remain identical for every new block created during the life-cycle of the platform, leading to an unlimited supply. The developers and advocates of this project assert that this will lead to a more stable price, making Dogecoin a more usable, and therefore credible, currency. However, it will take years to discover whether or not this is achieved.

However, regardless of the system, when investing in cryptocurrency it is vital to take tokenomics into consideration. Supply and demand are always critical in any financial system; this is one of the most broadly accepted principles in economics. This means that understanding factors that impact on supply and demand related to a cryptocurrency are vitally important to both developers and investors.

Given the flexible and diverse nature of cryptocurrency, this means that there can be several factors to consider. Use cases are particularly important - how specifically will the digital currency be utilized? Are there strong links between the usage of the platform, the services being constructed, and the underlying asset? How many coins or tokens are in circulation? How many will exist in the foreseeable future? What is the ownership model for the system, and are there plans to set aside some tokens or coins for developers? Is the platform stable, have users experienced any security issues, and are all tokens mined by the system usable?

The collective consideration of these factors is the lifeblood of tokenomics. By assessing these factors together, investors gain insight into how much assets may be worth in the foreseeable future. This is one of the reasons that use cases are so important with cryptocurrencies. Balancing all of these factors can be a tricky proposition, but this approach to the investment medium offers important insight into whether a particular asset has a bright outlook, or a brighter outlook than other comparable tokens.

CONCLUSION

In conclusion, it is difficult to do this subject justice in a single chapter, as there is so much possibility in the blockchain space, and so many different things happening. In many ways, the future of blockchain technology is completely unpredictable, considering that it can be utilized for almost anything, and many innovative people are currently working on delivering new use cases and concepts every day.

What should be clear is the difference between crypto coins and tokens. These two terms sound extremely similar, yet this chapter has conveyed the reality that their use cases are often wildly different. Most people would fundamentally understand the ethos behind cryptocurrency coins without the concept needing to be explained in any depth. But tokens have a much broader base of application, and are used in several different ways, depending on the system in question.

Ultimately, the only limit to the potential of the blockchain is the limit of human imagination. It is a technology that has the potential to go anywhere and achieve anything.

References

1. *Cornell Law School - Legal Information Institute.*

(1948). SECURITIES AND EXCHANGE COMMISSION v. W. J. HOWEY CO. et al.
2. Zmudzinski, A. (2019). Binance CEO CZ: Crypto Growth Needs Entrepreneurs and Projects, Not ETFs. *Yahoo!*.
3. *Investopedia*. (2019). TRON CEO Justin Sun on Blockchain and Scalability.

CHAPTER 4
SECURITY AND THE BLOCKCHAIN

ONE OF THE major issues that virtually everyone immediately associates with cryptocurrency and the blockchain is security. This isn't helped by some sensationalist, and often completely inaccurate, media stories and headlines. While these outlets are frequently using typical tactics to sell newspapers and garner attention, it ultimately can be quite misleading for people considering purchasing cryptocurrency for the first time.

There is something of a dichotomy at the heart of the security issue. On the one hand, a lot of the gossip related to this subject is borderline farcical! Conversely, it should also be noted that security is an important issue. It isn't something that should be neglected with cryptocurrencies, or indeed any investment or financial product. However, rather than paying heed to raucous media propaganda, if you're going to understand security and the blockchain, it is vital to be informed.

NEW PRINCIPLE

One of the first things to note about cryptocurrency security is that it creates what is virtually a new principle in the financial sector. Traditionally, any financial products are handled by huge institutions, and it is taken for granted that they will offer both security and protection. Frankly, the jury is out on how effectively this is actually implemented.

We all have the impression that our money is safe in a bank, but in reality if your account is hacked, it is extremely unlikely (I would say inevitable) that the bank will try to blame it on you! They will do anything and everything in order to avoid acknowledging that they made a mistake, even if you have done absolutely nothing wrong. This isn't always necessarily successful, but it is a process that you will have to go through in the unfortunate event that your account is ever hacked or stolen from.

Conversely, the blockchain and cryptocurrency puts a completely different mechanism in place. Any security provisions are created by the owner of the coins or tokens, and therefore you take complete responsibility for your own investment. If things go wrong with cryptocurrency, you are to blame, so the security of your tokens is only as strong as your own diligence. This is one of the many ways that cryptocurrency can be seen as a libertarian project; it places the onus on the individual rather than a centralized authority.

Some people shrink from this sort of responsibility, and others relish it. But what is clear is that there does need to be some form of security in place in order to secure your cryptocurrency tokens. For example, ask yourself this simple question...if you had 50 gold bars under your bed, would you feel safe leaving your house on a regular basis? Most people would not, as it is extremely difficult to get that quantity of gold adequately insured, and so it would always be vulnerable to theft.

ULTRA-SECURE PLATFORM

However, the good news is that the blockchain represents an ultra-secure platform, once you understand how it operates and what measures need to be put in place. Once you have tackled the process of managing security, your cryptocurrency tokens will be 100% secure. Arguably more secure than any other investment that has ever existed. However, in order to achieve this you do need to understand how blockchain and security works.

Blockchain technology produces highly structured data that possesses inherent qualities of security. It doesn't need anything extra to be added or built in to be secure; it is fundamentally secure by its very nature. Principles included in blockchain security are cryptography, decentralization and consensus. However, if you don't properly understand how blockchain security works, and fail to take the necessary measures to protect your crypto coins or tokens, then you can become vulnerable.

We've already explained the way that blockchain technology works in some depth in this book, so this chapter won't revisit old information. However, it is important to note that there are different types of blockchain, and these can make a difference to the security provisions required.

PUBLIC AND PRIVATE BLOCKCHAINS

Public blockchain networks enable anyone to join and participate in the processes associated with them. They use computers connected to the Internet in order to validate transactions and achieve consensus. Public blockchains are by far the most common available currently, and certainly every major project in the cryptocurrency niche is reliant on this form of blockchain.

Private blockchains utilize identity in order to confirm membership, and then confer privileges on these individuals or organizations. Effectively, only those people with special permissions can access and maintain the transaction ledger. Any private blockchain requires more identity and access controls, and the very nature of a private blockchain means that it is more tightly controlled. This offers compliance and regulatory advantages, but it can be restrictive in comparison to a public blockchain.

Most people reading this book, and indeed most people in the cryptocurrency space, will utilize a public blockchain most, if not all, of the time. The whole basis of Bitcoin, Ethereum and other cryptocurrency projects is that they are based on communities. It is therefore an absolute necessity for them to use public blockchain technology. As mentioned previously, this form of blockchain technology and cryptocurrency project then puts the emphasis on security in the hands of the individual.

This is a noble principle, but there are, of course, many nefarious individuals at large who will be more than willing to steal your cryptocurrency tokens. CNBC recently reported that global cybercrime could exceed $10 trillion annually by 2025.[1] While cryptocurrency is only a small proportion of this massive figure, the possibility of your tokens being stolen definitely shouldn't be dismissed.

WALLET TECHNOLOGY

Even if you're entirely new to cryptocurrencies, you have probably encountered the concept of wallets. These are central to cryptocurrency security, and can actually be physical devices, although they don't really resemble traditional wallets! In cryptocurrency, wallets can be both software and hardware devices, and choosing a wallet is generally dependent on the requirements of a consumer. Both approaches have advantages and disadvantages, and it is therefore worthwhile to briefly discuss these.

Software wallets are more readily accessible and flexible, often being stored online or via the cloud. This can make them attractive for investors that are only storing a relatively small amount of cryptocurrency, and need to access it on a regular basis. However, there is no doubt that hardware wallets, based on technology that is referred to as cold storage, can be considered the safest method for holding any cryptocurrency token. This technology is not accessible via the Internet, and is by definition much more difficult to crack. That doesn't mean that software wallets are necessarily unsafe, it just means that hardware wallets are universally recognized as being the safest way to store crypto tokens and coins.

Wallet technology is based on private keys. These are complex and lengthy passwords that are used to access tokens. Without a private key, it is impossible to access your cryptocurrency tokens, which helps with security. However, it should also be emphasized that without your private key, you won't be able to access your tokens either! So it's important to store your key in an extremely private place, but never to forget where you've stored it!

Online wallets are also referred to as hot wallets, and utilize Internet-connected devices, whether desktop computers, tablets, or smartphones. The reason that these can be more vulnerable than cold storage is that the private keys required to secure your tokens are generated online. While it is not likely that your private key will be intercepted, it is also not beyond the realm of possibility. There are unbelievably resourceful and knowledgeable computing experts in the hacking community, and the most innocuous information posted online can ultimately be disastrous. In this regard, one of the simplest and most fundamental principles regarding cryptocurrency investment is simply not to talk about it! Or certainly not online! Even alerting people on the Internet to the fact that you hold a great deal of cryptocurrency can attract hackers, and end in disaster.

Nonetheless, regardless of whether you are careful in this respect or not, there is no doubt that your cryptocurrency tokens will be safer in a cold storage wallet. And it is definitely not recommended to store cryptocurrency in an exchange. These are simply custodial accounts that are provided by platforms. While efforts are made to secure your tokens, the reality is that you never hold the private key associated with the cryptocurrency, and consequently you never take responsibility for your tokens. Many people do this perfectly safely without ever encountering any problems, but if there were an event in which an exchange is hacked and your account becomes compromised, your funds are surrendered. This is definitely not recommended!

EXCHANGE THEFTS

The risks of leaving your cryptocurrency in exchange storage cannot be overstated. In April, 2021, Fortune reported that there have been approximately $2.5 billion worth of cryptocurrency thefts in the last decade.[2] This amounts to a much greater figure once inflation is taken into consideration, probably in excess of $15 billion. Much of this figure has been purloined from exchanges, which means that you should definitely keep tokens in exchange accounts for the shortest period of time possible.

There are many hardware wallets available now, and most of these are USB drive devices that store private keys securely. They are kept completely separately from desktop computers, and are never connected to the Internet. This not only keeps them away from the web, it also ensures that they could never be infected by viruses or malware. In common with much of the cryptocurrency community, hardware devices are often open-source, meaning that the community associated with them can continue to enhance their safety, and indeed declare that they have been developed to an adequate standard.

The most important thing to remember is that if you lose your cryptocurrency tokens, you are basically fucked! There isn't anyone to contact! You can't call Ghostbusters or Interpol! The people that stole your tokens will never be seen again! That is why you have to absolutely prioritize cryptocurrency security. Having said that, I must emphasize again, if you do keep your tokens secure then there is absolutely no possibility whatsoever that they will ever be stolen. But any lackadaisical attitude on your behalf can definitely be punished, and it is your responsibility to take adequate steps. No one else will do this on your behalf.

BEST PRACTICES

With this in mind, there are a raft of best practices for security that you can put in place in order to prevent the private key for your cryptocurrency tokens ever being stolen. I would list the first of these are simply using a cold storage hardware wallet in the first place, as compromising on security in the cryptocurrency space is false economy and, frankly, a stupid idea!

You should also ensure that you opt for a solution that has two-factor authentication built-in. This will make it significantly more difficult to crack your wallet, even in the unlikely event that someone manages to steal your private key. You should choose a pin code that is impossible to guess, and which features a complex series of letters, numbers and characters. The more complex and less generic that your password is, the less chance of a computer cracking it via algorithms. If you use standard words, it is far easier for a supercomputer to hack your password.

Before committing to a hardware device, you should ensure that you've verified all of the information held. A degree of paranoia is essential in the cryptocurrency space, and you should ensure that your devices cannot be compromised. Don't reveal anything related to your crypto tokens in public - always ensure that this information remains strictly private.

Phishing sites are another important issue with cryptocurrency security. Regardless of the type of storage that you choose, there are many illegitimate websites that imitate exchanges with the intention of stealing your login and private key data. You must check carefully when using any website addresses, and also beware of any suspicious or unlikely email. It is quite rare for exchanges or other similar platforms to contact you via email, and certainly not in a generic fashion. The bottom line is that you must not click on anything unless you are 100% certain of its authenticity.

In line with this policy, it is essential to only access websites that possess a valid HTTPS certificate. There are even browser plug-ins that you can download, such as "HTTPS Everywhere", which stop your browser from accessing any other website whatsoever. It's also important to secure your WiFi connection, and to never connect with any critical security point via public WiFi. Frankly, this should never be necessary, but it is important to reiterate the importance of secure WiFi. Strong encryption, such as the WPA-2 protocol, is essential.

Other measures that you can implement include separating your funds, so that your crypto assets aren't all held in one place, and whitelisting IP and withdrawal addresses. You should use as many of these measures as possible, and ideally all of them. You can't take chances with security when it comes to utilizing cryptocurrency and blockchain platforms. Finally, make sure that you back-up your cryptocurrency wallet regularly, as this will protect you against hardware failure.

Your cryptocurrency is your responsibility, so never take shortcuts.

This chapter can come across as a little chilling! It's never pleasant to consider the fact that your hard-earned money and investments can be stolen. And the fact that cryptocurrency remains somewhat unfamiliar to a lot of people can create uncertainty. It somehow seems less solid than the money that we grew up with. So it's important to place all of these issues into context.

Firstly, theft is just part of life. One day, we will all hopefully reside in a utopia, in which there is no need for anyone to steal anything, and everyone is a wonderful human being! Until that time, which doesn't appear to be on the horizon currently, we have to assume that many people will continue to engage in criminal activity. There is a vast amount of money to be made from financial theft, and cryptocurrencies are definitely one legitimate target. Many of the organized criminals involved in targeting cryptocurrencies are sociopaths and psychopaths, and they ultimately do not care whatsoever about the consequences of their actions. This is just a reality that we all have to live with, just as we lock our doors in the morning and evening to prevent burglary.

It's also important to understand that the amount of cryptocurrency theft is relatively trivial compared to many other aspects of cybercrime. I've already quoted the total value of the cybercrime worldwide in this chapter; it is an astronomical figure. At the time of writing, cryptocurrency remains an entirely trivial proportion of the overall figure associated with cybercrime, and this is unlikely to change in the foreseeable future.

The United Nations estimates that $2 trillion is laundered on an annual basis, in association with organized crime.[3] In September, 2020, the *Washington Post* reported on the extent of this money laundering, in an article entitled: "Global banks process trillions in dirty money despite suspicions, investigation finds". The story noted that "trillions of dollars in money connected to criminal activity are sloshing through global banks. The banks and US authorities know it, and they're not doing nearly enough to stop it."[4] Of course, they don't stop it because they want the business. That's the most optimistic spin that you can possibly put on the situation!

It's important to note here that these are the institutions that we entrust with the safety of our money. Unfortunately, there is no little or no basis for this trust. It gives me no pleasure to report this reality, but failing to report it wouldn't stop it from being the case. Yet because the system is familiar, and because its proponents are extremely powerful, we somehow invest a level of credibility and legitimacy in it that is completely undeserved.

Theft is normal. Theft is institutionalized. We therefore have to expect there to be a certain degree of theft in the cryptocurrency marketplace, while also understanding that it is a drop in the ocean compared to the system that we were inculcated into from our cradles. It's also important to remember that cryptocurrency provides us with the opportunity to take control of our own tokens. There are protections built into blockchains and cryptocurrency products that are completely watertight. They can never be broken. Indeed, this is one of the most compelling reasons why we need to be careful with our own private keys!

But once you have mastered the art of keeping your cryptocurrency safe, you can rest assured that it is absolutely 100% secure. It will never be stolen. It can never be compromised. It is completely uncrackable and unhackable.

Don't ever let anyone tell you that about conventional money. Because it's simply not true.

References

1. *CNBC*. (2021). Cybercrime could cost $10.5 trillion dollars by 2025, according to Cybersecurity Ventures.
2. Tully, S. (2021). These are the largest cyber thefts of the past decade—and 80% of them involve Bitcoin. *Fortune*.

3. *United Nations Office on Drugs and Crime*. (2021). Money Laundering.
4. Newmyer, T. (2020). The Finance 202: Global banks process trillions in dirty money despite suspicions, investigation finds. *The Washington Post*.

CHAPTER 5
DECENTRALIZED APPLICATIONS - WHAT ARE THEY AND WILL THE EXPERIENCE BE THE SAME?

APPS HAVE BECOME an important part of most people's lives, particularly younger generations. The vast popularity of mobile platforms has led to billions of global app downloads every year. The global app market is expected to be worth over $6 trillion in 2021, with the average user spending over $1,000 annually on mobile software.[1]

The major beneficiaries of this have been the behemoths of Apple and Google, thanks to their well-established app stores. In 2020, Google Play Services became the first app to be downloaded 10 billion times,[2] while Apple's market capitalization climbing over $2 trillion can be mainly attributed to its success in the mobile and app marketplaces.[3]

Another significant aspect of the app revolution is the speed of adoption involved. Driven by millennials and young people, smartphones and their attendant app technology have established themselves as part of the mainstream culture with a rapidity that has never been witnessed previously. Smartphones achieved 70% adoption in the US population within just six years of their initial release, and worldwide usage of apps had already reached 1.6 trillion hours annually by 2016.[4].

THE DUOPOLY

The dual-dominance of Apple and Google over this burgeoning platform has also been quite apparent. While Google has its fingers in many successful pies, the expansion of its app business has been exponential. Gross revenue at the Google App Store increased by over 250% between 2016 and 2020,[5] and people all over the world now rely on this platform for both entertainment and more utilitarian motivations. The story is the same at Apple, with 255% growth in App Store revenue over the same period ensuring that it comfortably topped $100 billion by 2020.[6]

This has led to a duopoly of the operating system market, with few serious pretenders to the thrones occupied by Apple's proprietary iOS and Google's Android contender. This has certainly been commercially beneficial for Apple and Google, but it has also arguably led to stagnation in the market. Both Google and, particularly, Apple have been criticized for creating platforms that are closed ecosystems, guilty of stymying creativity; hence the phenomenon of 'jailbreaking' Apple devices to enable more user freedom (even though this is vehemently discouraged by Apple).

Both companies have made liberating changes to their operating systems in recent years, in an attempt to alleviate this opprobrium. But the impression still remains that the Google Play Store, the Apple App Store, Android and iOS are closed shops; tolerant of developers, but never really aligning themselves with the creative community enthusiastically. Whether this is a fair commentary or not is debatable – and there is no doubt that both Apple and Google would defend their conduct, and celebrate their successes, ardently – but what isn't open to debate is the fact that the two megacorporations will always retain strong central control over their ecosystems and the related app community.

KEY ADVANTAGE

It probably won't have escaped your notice that this ethos is the polar opposite of the one that is advocated by cryptocurrencies. And this baton has now been picked up by dApps, which promise to address many of the problems associated with the existing app climate.

The key advantage of decentralized apps is precisely that they are decentralized; open and permissionless, meaning that they can't be controlled by a central entity. This certainly doesn't apply to traditional apps; indeed, Apple and Google both restrict the allowable content on their platforms quite stringently. This would never be possible with dApps; as they are built on blockchains, there is simply no centralized owner that could restrict or take control of any decentralized application.

Furthermore, the open source nature of dApps, coupled with this freedom, means that they have possibilities beyond their unrestricted nature. Developers can effectively collaborate with dApps, building on top of one another's work, and creating exciting projects based on the input of several contributors. This provides the potential to combine different elements from various projects to create new types of applications and services; a positive evolution in what is already an important and culture-shifting field.

Decentralized apps are already attracting an active community of developers, and this will expand massively in the future, as the audience for the innovation grows. Considering the vast range of apps that exist on the Google Play Store and Apple App Store platforms, which can expect hundreds of thousands of dApps to emerge eventually, not least because there will be far less restrictions placed on those parties interested in creating them.

Accessing dApps will be somewhat different from the way that users interact with traditional apps. In order to comprehend this, it's first necessary to understand how dApps work. Decentralized applications comprise a suite of smart contracts that interact with one another autonomously, once the developers have deployed them on a blockchain. Ethereum has become a market-leader in this niche, but, as we've discussed previously, there are other competitors available as well.

In order to access Ethereum dApps, an Ethereum wallet that can interact with smart contracts is required. Trust Wallet is one of the most prominent examples at the time of writing. Accessing the wallet involves a relatively straightforward process, and then you are good to go with dApps. As the field grows, there will be a range of options available, and these will all be accessible from one portal, much as is the case with existing app stores.

IMPORTANCE OF AGNOSTICISM

Agnosticism will also be an important concept with dApps. This is a simple concept; agnosticism merely refers to a single blockchain platform that enables multiple different blockchains. This is vital for the development of decentralized apps, as this agnostic quality will make it possible to open up decentralized applications to various protocols. This is important, as the many use cases associated with the technology will require differing performance characteristics, which are unlikely to be provided by a solitary blockchain. Anything that enables more flexibility will be a major positive for the future of dApps.

As the adoption of the blockchain continues to expand, it is inevitable that decentralized applications will gain increased attraction. The advantages for businesses of building decentralized customer experiences, and more fluid commerce climates, will become increasingly obvious and more prominent. Considering the direction of this business application, it is therefore important for companies to consider how they can design and implement dApps effectively, as the ethos behind commerce shifts towards a decentralized model.

Although dApps have yet to hit the mainstream, they are growing rapidly in both number and popularity. It's important to remember that the blockchain and cryptocurrency was considered an obscure innovation at first, but has become a market with trillions of dollars in capitalization. So the adoption of dApps may be relatively steady, but it can quickly gain momentum as more people get on board with the concept. This should be easier and more quick than the cryptocurrency revolution, as there are so many more people already aware of the potential of decentralized applications than was the case with cryptos when Bitcoin was conceived.

MULTIPLE USE CASES

Use cases for dApps are multiple, and there are already an array of apps available. But the first products to really make an impression on the market could come in the fields of healthcare, content creation, games, and the arts. There is a particularly compelling case for dApps in any field that requires widespread access to a mass database or system, which means that many expect decentralized applications to become particularly popular in healthcare. This is especially true considering that eHealth software is already a maturing space, expected to be worth nearly $200 billion annually by 2025.[7] Popular fields such as games and content creation are also likely to receive a boost from the democratized nature of the dApps in the short-term, with the younger consumers associated with these fields likely to embrace decentralized applications more quickly.

It's difficult, though, to say precisely when dApps will explode, and become part of the mainstream. Kyle Lu, CEO of Dapp.com, shared data and charts on the deployment of dApps with *Coin Telegraph*, and told the publication that "you could see that it is a good trend of usage climbing as more dapps were built and more users are engaging."

dApps aren't a new phenomenon; in fact, they've been around for several years. This means that there are trends and patterns available on the development of the niche, and these have been closely followed by insiders such as Lu. Dapp.com has been closely monitoring the market for nearly 5 years at the time of writing, and Lu continued his conversation by pointing out that "the main reason driving interest and usage of DApps is innovation of business models — all the 'hype' in the DApp area is driven by businesses and products delivered in a way that people haven't seen before."[8]

Data on the development of dApps indicates that the number of applications has increased five-fold between 2017 and 2021, while the number of users has experienced vast exponential growth. There are now millions of users of decentralized apps, 4 million regular users according to Dapp.com data, whereas this figure was well under 1 million back in 2017. This shows how quickly the concept is growing, and how more users are coming online as the benefits of decentralized applications become more apparent.

ADDRESSING SECURITY

If there is one issue that dApps need to address it is the oft-asserted quibble that improvements need to be made to user experience and ease of access. While accessing decentralized applications isn't necessarily complicated, it still remains more complex than the process associated with traditional apps. There can also be improvements made to user interfaces and the overall experience associated with dApps, and this will be critical in the continuing maturation of the field.

There are already innovative products available in the dApps space, but the history of technology has repeatedly demonstrated that it isn't the most powerful or flexible technology that is successful, it is the most accessible and affordable that typically dominates the market. This is food for thought for those advocating and involved with the dApps revolution, and an issue that definitely needs to be addressed before mainstream adoption is achieved.

Furthermore, there are still security issues associated with decentralized apps. Because dApps cannot be controlled by a single server, they don't create data silos or a single point of failure, making them slightly more vulnerable to attacks. Already some of the security problems associated with decentralized apps have been addressed, with new methods of ensuring security and account recovery assisting with the on-boarding of users in existing platforms. But there is still more work to do.

However, developers do face something of a conundrum in this area. While the security issues associated with dApps can be solved, it is difficult to divert the required budget into this area until mass adoption of dApps is achieved. But it is harder to achieve mass adoption until the security is beefed up; a catch-22 situation that might not be solved overnight.

Nonetheless, most market observers and analysts following the industry closely believe that it's just a matter of time before mass adoption occurs. When dApps are as accessible as traditional applications, while also delivering the advantages of a blockchain, the use case for dApps will be so compelling that critical mass will inevitably be achieved. The massive increase in the prominence and utilization of blockchain also provides a compelling and receptive audience for these dApps products, and one that already understands the arguments and principles involved.

Indeed, some of the experts in this field believe that within a matter of years consumers won't even realize that they are using platforms powered by blockchain technology. Jon Jordan, communications director at DappRadar, commented to *Coin Telegraph* that new blockchain applications "won't even promote themselves as using the blockchain", and that a new type of user experience will be created for applications that far outweighs anything that has been achieved previously.

dApps will be all about democratization, diversity, interaction and community. Essentially, many of the qualities that are trumpeted by the developers of existing app platforms, and the corporations that develop them, but which are rarely delivered in reality. Dapps will be very attractive for people of a libertarian persuasion, as it will be impossible for a central actor to limit the scope of these software packages. dApps will simply proceed in the direction that their communities desire, which is an exciting prospect considering the limitations that can be placed on existing apps by trillion-dollar businesses.

MAINSTREAM ACCEPTANCE

In fact, the mainstream acceptance of dApps as a concept could be accelerated by the plans of 40 of the world's largest financial institutions. JPMorgan and Credit Suisse are among the major names involved in a consortium that is currently investigating the potential of the blockchain to deliver faster and more secure transactions. This sort of news is massive for the future of the blockchain, and could in turn have a knock-on effect on the adoption of dApps.

The reason that major financial sector players are interested in the blockchain is its ability to deliver improvements and efficiency savings in a wide variety of industries. The potential of the blockchain has been particularly prominent in finance, but it is also believed that it can deliver improvements in such fields as power, healthcare, real estate, tourism, transport, and many others. There is no doubt that major financial institutions would love to have a solution that they can implement across several business areas, improving profitability and working practices as a result.

This would then lead to a future in which dApps become rapidly more viable, as companies of this magnitude would be able to invest the money required in order to solve some of the security and user base issues. As more mainstream organizations recognize the importance and potential of the blockchain, all of its related products will begin to come to the fore, and dApps will begin a revolution that will completely change the face of software and applications.

There is no doubt that this future is approaching rapidly. The only thing in doubt is when precisely it will arrive. As with everything in the world of blockchain, early adopters will no doubt benefit most.

References

1. Perez, S. (2017). App economy to grow to $6.3 trillion in 2021, user base to nearly double to 6.3 billion. *TechCrunch*.
2. *Times of India*. (2020). This is the first Android app to cross 10 billion downloads.
3. Burztyntsky, J. (2020). Apple becomes first U.S. company to reach a $2 trillion market cap. *CNBC*.
4. Scopelliti, R. (2018). Youthquake 4.0: A Whole Generation and the Industrial Revolution, pp. 24. *Marshall Cavendish International*.
5. *Statista*. (2021). Worldwide gross app revenue of Google Play from 2016 to 2020.
6. Iqbal, M. (2021). App Revenue Data (2021). *Business of Apps*.
7. *Research and Markets*. (2021). The Worldwide eHealth Industry is Expected to Reach $193.8 Billion by 2025.
8. Jenkinson, G. (2020). DApps Need to Nail Usability to Move From Crypto Niche to Mainstream. *Coin Telegraph*.

CHAPTER 6
BUYING A PIECE OF ART OR A FOOTBALL SHIRT AS A DIGITAL ASSET - IT MIGHT NOT BE THAT CRAZY!

ASIDE FROM THE artistic expression that we associate with paintings, music, literature and other forms of art, the field has also long since represented a platform for commodification. Successful art is worth big money, whether it's The Beatles or Picasso. Therefore, the idea of artwork being potentially worth millions of dollars is nothing new. But the blockchain, and its related technologies, are revolutionizing this concept, and hugely widening the scope of what can be considered valuable.

This is being made possible by non-fungible tokens (NFTs). We briefly touched upon this concept previously in the book, but in this chapter we're going to explore the intriguing possibilities offered by this innovation.

WHAT IS FUNGIBILITY?

Firstly, it is important to understand the concept of fungibility itself, as this is not part of the everyday lexicon of language. In short, a fungible asset is something that can be easily interchanged. The obvious example of this would be money, whereby anyone and everyone is aware that you can swap a $10 note for two $5 dollar notes, and you have performed an equal exchange.

Conversely, if something is non-fungible, such an exchange is impossible. It cannot be readily interchanged with something else; it is unique. Examples of this could range from a property, through famous paintings, to music, to really anything that you can imagine. Simply what makes such an asset non-fungible is its inability to be readily exchanged.

NFT tokens make it possible to acquire such unique assets, by storing data on a digital ledger. NFTs can be used to represent an almost unquantifiable diversity of assets, but are typically focused on photos, videos, audio, and other types of digital files. Blockchain technology is used in order to establish verifiable and public proof of ownership, although copies of the original file can also be distributed.

EARLY NFTS

The concept of NFTs took some time to arise. NFTs weren't baked into the early blockchain cake; the first project associated with this technology was launched in 2015 - seven years after the first Bitcoin white paper was released. Again, the flexibility of the Ethereum blockchain has proved important in this field, and is set to play a major role in the growth of NFT technology. Interest in the concept has grown as cryptocurrencies have similarly expanded in notoriety, and sales in NFT tokens exceeded $2 billion in the first quarter of 2021.[1]

NFTs are data, but this data can be associated with a particular digital physical asset. A license can then be associated with the asset, and the NFT can be traded and sold on digital markets. While such digital markets remain embryonic, they are also growing in number and prominence rapidly. The value of the NFT market has exploded in recent months, and there is increasing awareness and enthusiasm about the concept of purchasing digital assets and art.

While headlines have been made by the multi-million dollar deals associated with NFTs, this is another aspect of the blockchain revolution that is truly liberalizing. NFT tokens can be created by anyone, for consumption by anyone, and they can represent virtually anything that can be conceived or imagined.

UNIQUE VALUE

However, while NFTs can be copied, it is important to note that the original retains a unique value; similar to the way that prints can be made of expensive paintings, but they never carry the financial cachet of the original. This is why a digital certificate of ownership is attached to an original NFT digital asset, as a mark of ownership and commercial merit.

While they are particularly associated with traditional art and popular culture, NFT tokens can be utilized across an incredibly wide variety of fields. The digital assets can be used in order to create anything of real value, whether that is digital content, items related to video games, tickets to a real-world event, virtual worlds and related creations, or even in the deeds or titles associated with physical property. That shortlist merely scratches the surface of what is possible, and already NFT tokens have proven to be hugely valuable in numerous areas, while offering a unique way to take physical ownership of a digital asset or work.

If great figures from the world of art or classical music, such as Vincent van Gogh and Wolfgang Amadeus Mozart were around today, there is no doubt that they would now be contemplating the NFT revolution! Some big names have moved to create non-fungible examples of their work, and this is set to accelerate in the future as the niche becomes increasingly mainstream. One of the most successful examples of this was when the musician Grimes sold some examples of her digital art for the eye-watering figure of $6 million.

And this is just the beginning. NFT tokens have yet to become part of everyday life for most people, but there is a huge and enthusiastic community of people following the technology. With reference to the title of the chapter, sport is one of the fields that has particularly benefited from NFT, with some of the biggest names in the field already taking advantage of the platform and opportunities offered by blockchain innovation.

SPORT SALES

For example, the Italian soccer club Fiorentina have launched blockchain-based merchandise with the limited edition digital NFT offer of 95 new jerseys; representing the 95 years that the club has existed.[2] This is just one example of shirts being made available through digital NFT technology, with the Football Shirt Collective noting that an incredible range of concept jerseys can now be made available, as NFT has provided an exciting platform for designers to showcase and sell their creations. The technology associated with the blockchain and NFT also means that content creators can continue to receive percentages on future sales of their creations; a win-win for the creative community.

Arguably the world's greatest footballer has also strongly aligned himself with the NFT market. An NFT related to Lionel Messi, of Paris Saint-Germain and Argentina, has already sold for in excess of $1 million on the Ethernity NFT marketplace.[3] The NFT, which depicts Messi travelling on a meteorite, is just one of several official Messi tokens available, with the Ethernity platform dubbing the selection of NFTs as "The Messiverse".

NBA owner Mark Cuban has also moved into the NFT space, supporting a startup by the name of Eternal that intends to capture some of the most important clips from online streamers. This effectively amalgamates two growing trends; the popularity of the blockchain and the explosion in viewership of new online media platforms. Cuban is one of several investors who have collectively offered $4.5 million to the project, with Eternal currently focused on the most popular streamers on the Twitch platform.[4]

IMPORTANCE OF TWITCH

Twitch is an ideal partner for NFT technology, considering its massive appeal to young people, and the fertile gaming culture that has been developed by the

Amazon-owned site. One of the major beneficiaries of Twitch's increasing popularity has been chess, with the ancient board game having experienced a completely unpredicted exponential growth in the last 18 months. Chess streamers and content creators are pushing the boundaries of the royal game, and this has also led the sport to participate in the growing NFT revolution.

This was recognized when the world's first NFT chess trophy was recently awarded to world champion Magnus Carlsen, following his victory in the Meltwater Champions Chess Tour.[5] Chess has been quick to embrace the innovations offered by the blockchain, with a major tournament recently paying the winner, American Wesley So, in cryptocurrency. Carlsen commented: "It's a nice trophy and I'm very happy to be breaking this ground."

NEWS NFTS

Sport has been a major platform for the growth and expansion of NFT, but items of particular historical interest are also worthy of serious consideration. There have already been several examples of newsworthy historical precedents being captured in NFT form, and then being sold to interested parties.

For example, Tim Berners-Lee, often described as the inventor of the World Wide Web, sold some of the original source code associated with the Internet for $5.4 million.[6] Auctioned at the world-famous Sotheby's, the code attracted over 50 bids. Meanwhile, Jack Dorsey, Twitter's founder and CEO, also auctioned off an NFT token featuring the world's first ever tweet. This historical curiosity raised $2.9 million.[7] And Twitter has moved to participate more regularly with NFTs; giving away 140 non-fungible tokens through the marketplace Rarible.

The news network CNN has also recognized the value of NFT tokens, announcing in June its intention to launch "Vault by CNN". This innovative concept will feature some of the most momentous moments from the 41-year history of the cable news channel. These include space shuttle launches, election-related reports and the launch of CNN itself.[8] The vault continues to grow, and there is no doubt that CNN will digitally document many of the most important landmarks in the world, and particularly, US history.

This opens up the tantalizing proposition that major news will become regular NFT commodities in the future. This is intriguing, when one considers how sought after certain newspaper front pages become over time. Now they will become far more accessible, with the opportunity for people all over the world to own mementos of historic events.

MUSIC NFTS

Popular music has also got on board with NFT tokens, with rapper Jay-Z having sold a non-fungible token based on the album cover of his debut album, "Reasonable Doubt."[9] A representative of Sotheby's told Coindesk that the rap innovator was the ideal pioneer for this medium. "It's fitting that 'JAY-Z' pioneering lyrical brilliance is commemorated through the iconic vision of acclaimed artist Derrick Adams in a bold new medium," Cassandra Hatton commented. "The release of Heir to the Throne marks the continued influence of Reasonable Doubt and its deep legacy of cultural importance," Hatton continued. While on the subject of the auction house, it is also notable that Sotheby's has made cryptocurrency available as a payment method.

Taylor Swift is another major name featured in the Celebrity NFT collection from OMNI, which captures over 100 of the most popular names in show business. The plan of OMNI is to mint 2,000 NFT tokens, featuring the top 100 celebrities according to their rankings.[10]

However, NFT and blockchain technology doesn't just offer the possibility of enshrining famous musicians, it also provides a potential distribution network for music itself. Musicians can potentially tokenize and publish their work as NFT tokens, retaining copyright and creating a new distribution medium that is separate from often criticized platforms such as Spotify and Tidal. Whether or not that criticism is always fair, the fact remains that many artists believe that the share of revenue that they receive from such digital platforms is minimal, and NFTs therefore represent an attractive proposition, certainly for the most popular recording parties.

And people producing art outside of the established channels can hugely benefit from NFT digital distribution. Currently, in order for a song, or indeed any piece of art, to become successful it must be accepted by mainstream media. This is obviously limited to a select group of artists, which has led to the plurality of music available in the mainstream diminishing rapidly. By recording and distributing via NFT tokens, it becomes possible for more artists to reach an audience, and for a piece of music to go viral simply because it is well-received by the NFT community. This will potentially break the stranglehold that the major labels, digital platforms, and recording artist organizations currently have over the music industry. The rock band Kings of Leon has already become a pioneer in this area, becoming the first recording artist to announce the release of a new album, "When You See Yourself", in the form of an NFT. This was hugely successful, generating over $2 million in sales.

Already, it has been reported that NFT musical recordings have provided massive opportunities for artists during the Covid pandemic, which have resulted in revenues for the music industry falling by around 85%.[11] This has helped an array of smaller artists, while some big names have also raked in huge figures via NFT technology. For example, electronic dance musician 3LAU sold a collection of 33 NFTs that commemorated the three-year anniversary of his Ultraviolet album for over $11 million. Eminem is another big name that has embraced NFTs, with his "Shady Con" project offering some original instrumental beats and a set of action figures via NFT marketplace Nifty Gateway.[12]

MOVIES AND NFT

The film industry has also begun to embrace NFT technology. 20th Century Fox released a series of limited-edition digital posters to promote the movie Deadpool 2.[13] And the first movie release to be auctioned as an NFT has already emerged; Adam Benzine's 2015 documentary Claude Lanzmann: Spectres of the Shoah used the Rarible platform to achieve this.[14]

Other pioneering efforts have also been created. An NFT associated with the score of the movie Triumph was minted as the first NFT for a feature film score.[15] Zero Contact, directed by Rick Dugdale and starring Anthony Hopkins,[16] will also be released as an NFT, and there are a variety of other NFT projects in film also on the horizon.

DIGITAL ART

Art is another growing field within the NFT niche, with Mike Winkelmann, known professionally as Beeple, having sold an NFT featuring a collage of images from his "Everydays" series for over $69 million. This figure ensured that the collage became the fourth-most expensive artwork by a living artist, when it was auctioned via the infamous Christie's.[17]

Digital art was one of the earliest use cases for NFT, due to the specific ability of blockchain technology to deliver unique signatures and ownership. This has allowed many independent creators to copyright their work effectively, enabling independent distribution and profitability. Other prominent artists that have turned to the NFT platform in order to sell their wares include Krista Kim and Erwin Wurm.

OTHER PLATFORMS

Academia has also begun to embrace the growth in NFTs, with the University of California, Berkeley, recently announcing an auction for several NFT products. Patent disclosures for two Nobel Prize-winning inventions - CRISPR-Cas9 gene editing and cancer immunotherapy - will be sold to raise funds for the educational establishment, but the University will continue to own the patents for the inventions. When auctioned, the NFTs raised over $55,000.[18]

NFT tokens can also offer opportunities in digital collectables, ticketing, and in-game assets. One particularly interesting use of the technology has been to create virtual worlds, which can effectively become private members clubs based on NFT ownership. Virtual worlds such as Decentraland, Sandbox, CryptoVoxels and Somnium Space have also made it possible for users to create galleries of arts, clothes, real estate and other valuable items, while attending live events alongside a community of interested parties. This real estate has already become valuable, with a plot of virtual land representing approximately 16 acres on Decentraland being sold for over $900,000 in June 2021.[19]

POTENTIAL FOR CREATORS

While the large amounts of money generated by certain NFT transactions inevitably attract attention, this technology also offers long-term potential for creators in a wide variety of spaces. NFT and blockchain make it far more possible for people to copyright and distribute their creations, and this can then be applied to almost any field imaginable.

NFT tokens are completely non-geographical, meaning that you can purchase an asset based on the other side of the world and instantly have proof of ownership. Household names such as Amazon and eBay have changed the way that goods are sold and distributed, but NFT takes this to a whole new level, instantly connecting sellers with a marketplace that is global in scope.

Indeed, the rapid growth in the sale of NFT tokens means that a wealth of marketplaces has already sprung up. And the prominence of these marketplaces will only increase. It will become commonplace to buy, sell and exchange tokens, and NFT transactions will become part of everyday life. There has been a significant amount of investment and development in this area already; for example, the Bank of New York Mellon reported in June 2021 on Google's investment in NFT marketplaces, and the general potential of the niche.[20]

NFT technology is perhaps the most exciting innovation related to blockchain, as it opens up a world of transactions, interactions and creations that have never been possible previously. NFT has already been enthusiastically embraced by sellers and consumers alike, and the technology will create both a vibrant marketplace and huge opportunities for creative people.

References

1. Frank, R. (2021). NFT sales top $2 billion in first quarter, with twice as many buyers as sellers. *CNBC*.
2. *Inside World Football*. (2021). Fiorentina launch 95 NFT shirts using Genuino blockchain technology.
3. Yordanova, H. (2021). Lionel Messi NFT Sold for $1 million on Ethernity. *dAppRadar*.
4. Matney, L. (2021). Mark Cuban and Coinbase back Eternal, an NFT marketplace for trading Twitch streamer clips. *TechCrunch*.
5. Watson, L. (2021). Magnus Carlsen receives world's first NFT chess trophy. *Champions Chess Tour*.
6. Seward, Z. (2021). Berners-Lee NFT Sells for $5.4M at Sotheby's. *CoinDesk*.
7. *Ledger Insights*. (2021). Jack Dorsey sells his first tweet as an NFT for $2.9 million.
8. Weprin, A. (2021). CNN to Sell NFTs of Its Historic News Coverage. *Hollywood Reporter*.
9. Blistein, J. (2021). Jay-Z to Celebrate 25th Anniversary of 'Reasonable Doubt' by Selling First NFT. *Rolling Stone*.
10. Richard, I. (2021). OMNI to Launch Celebrity NFT Art Featuring Jay-Z, Taylor Swift, Elon

Musk, and MORE; Sale Starts on September. *TechTimes*.
11. Savage, M. (2020). Musicians will lose two-thirds of their income in 2020. *BBC*.
12. Kaufman, G. (2021). Eminem's First NFT Drop, 'Shady Con,' Includes One-of-a-Kind Slim Shady-Produced Beats. *Billboard*.
13. Heal, J. (2019). Deadpool posters can now be bought as NFTs. *Yahoo!*.
14. Ravindran, M. (2021). NFT Craze Enters Film World: 'Claude Lanzmann' Documentary is First Oscar Nominee to Be Released as Digital Token. *Variety*.
15. Finn, J. (2021). World's First Movie Score & Soundtrack For Sale As An NFT. *Screen Rant*.
16. Neale, M. (2021). Anthony Hopkins' new film 'Zero Contact' to debut on NFT platform. *New Musical Express*.
17. Kastrenakes, J. (2021). Beeple sold an NFT for $69 million. *The Verge*.
18. Decker, S. (2021). Nobel-Prize-Winning Data Is Focus of Berkeley NFT Contest. *Yahoo!*.
19. Howcroft, E. (2021). Virtual real estate plot sells for close to $1 million. *Reuters*.
20. Kehoe. L. & Twainy, Z. (2021). Venture Capital Investment in NFT Marketplaces. *Bank of New York Mellon*.

CHAPTER 7
FACEBOOK GETTING IN ON THE ACTION! AND WHY THAT MAY NOT BE A GOOD THING EVEN THOUGH WE 'LOVE' FACEBOOK!

WHILE BANKS and financial institutions were natural adversaries to the crypto revolution, at least in the early days, the same hasn't necessarily applied to the big tech companies. In many ways, the founders of the giants of the technology industry, most notably Google, Amazon, Facebook and Apple, shared something of a pioneering spirit with those who planted the first blockchains seeds. They were cut from similar cloth, and shared something of a modernizing outlook on business and life.

EARLY MOVES

In fact, all of this GAFA quartet, as they are often referred to collectively, have been linked with moves to legitimize cryptocurrency, as the sphere becomes ever more influential. In August, 2021, an article 'on' *Inc.com* outlined the compelling reasons why the powerful retailer may accept cryptocurrency payments in the foreseeable future, and go further still by launching its own blockchain.[1] The financial and organizational benefits of this are obvious for Amazon, particularly as the company already has a reputation for disrupting industries.

Apple has also been strongly linked with crypto, with Forbes reporting that the company is toying with the idea of accepting some of the top cryptos for payments,[2] particularly after a job advert emerged that specifically mentions "strategic alternative payment partners".[3] And Google has all of the data expertise required to really excel in the blockchain space. There have been few public pronouncements from the information giant on cryptos, but the move of its subsidiary, Alphabet, to partner with Theta Labs indicates a warmth towards the blockchain concept. Theta is a venture-backed blockchain company, which agreed a deal that sees Google Cloud enable users to deploy and run nodes from Theta's blockchain network.[4]

But it is Facebook that has been the most enthusiastic of the four tech giants when it comes to cryptocurrency, planning its own product in the shape of Diem. This project first began at Facebook in 2017, when the company started to develop a blockchain initiative internally. Facebook vice president David A. Marcus moved from Facebook Messenger to a new blockchain division in May, 2018, as reports of the social media company planning a cryptocurrency began to emerge.

Since then, Facebook has steadily ramped up on the project, and formally announced Diem (branded 'Libra' at that time) on June 18, 2019. Initially planned for release in 2020, the concept has been subject to delay, but it is clear from reports and Facebook statements that the corporation remains committed to releasing a proprietary cryptocurrency.

FINANCIAL BACKING

Facebook plans for the Diem token to be backed by financial assets, most likely baskets of currencies and US Treasury securities. In September 2019, Facebook had announced that the reserve basket would be made up of: 50% United States dollar, 18% Euro, 14% Japanese yen, 11% Pound sterling and 7% Singapore dollar,[5] although this has yet to be officially finalized, considering the unpredictable economic and currency climate. This means that Diem is not necessarily an investment token; Diem much more readily qualifies for the description of being a 'stablecoin'. These are cryptocurrencies that are backed by reserve assets. Because these coins are pegged directly to a non-virtual currency, they tend to fluctuate in value less dramatically than other cryptos.

The advantages of a cryptocurrency project for Facebook are quite obvious. Facebook is one of the world's biggest online businesses, and also one that operates entirely in cyberspace. There is no Facebook business outside of the Internet, and this means that it is entirely reliant on digital payments. The notion of developing its own currency is therefore an attractive one, and no doubt that this is one of the major motivations for the Diem Project.

FACEBOOK IMAGE

However, there is a catch. Most people involved in cryptocurrency would be understandably suspicious of any major company engaging in a crypto project, as it would seem to fly in the face of the whole do-it-yourself crypto ethos. Although cryptocurrency has made big money for many people, it has always been driven by enthusiasts, rather than cynical venture capitalists. But in the case of Facebook, there are even more compelling reasons for people to be suspicious.

The Diem project isn't just about money, it's also about information. Data is extremely important to Facebook, indeed it is the primary currency of the platform. Facebook already holds an almost incalculable quantity of customer data, and this is used to profile users in a way that could be considered manipulative. The company actively attempts to steer users in the direction of certain advertising clients, in order to finance the platform. Facebook itself engages in extensive PR in order to make this process seem anything but invasive, but it could never legally deny the fact that this is its primary business operation. This is just how Facebook makes money. If it didn't do this, it would never have become a profitable company. When it talks about privacy, it is little short of nonsense; its business is reliant on invading your privacy!

The data held by Facebook on people all over the world is quite extensive, particularly for users who have engaged with the platform regularly. Hopefully, most people are aware that direct data, the basic information that you add to your Facebook account during your activity on the website, is stored by the company. I'm sure that there are many naive people who have never considered this, or not considered it seriously, but hopefully everyone reading this book is at least aware of this concept! In short, names, ages, marital status, places of residence, employment, education, and countless other personal details of billions of people are already held by Facebook.

STORING DATA

But that's just the beginning. All of your Facebook activity is also stored by the company. This includes all of the pages, pictures and statuses that you've liked, any groups that you've joined, links and videos that you shared to your newsfeed, and countless other facets of the website. By storing all of this information, Facebook is building up a surprisingly detailed picture on all of its users.

And it doesn't stop there. Social media sites such as Facebook can use cookies to track your activity on websites outside of their own. There is an unbelievable amount of information generated via this practice, and this can be then used to create a targeted campaign for every individual user. This is why advertising has become so sophisticated, and the reason why the Internet seems to know more about you than you know about yourself!

Many people may not be particularly concerned by this. We seem to have accepted the fact that massive companies are spying on us with an acquiescence that can perhaps be considered alarming! However, it is vital to understand why this is important in relation to the Diem project, and why many members of the cryptocurrency community are extremely sceptical about the concept of a Facebook blockchain and crypto.

The Diem project can be used as an extra layer of information, which can be used to further control the individual and what they see online. Marketing can be targeted with ever greater detail, and the project can impose an almost insidious influence over people's daily lives. Meanwhile, this information will be linked to WhatsApp, Instagram, and God knows what else! While state snooping into private data has been extensive - for example, as revealed by Edward Snowden - there is no government on the planet that holds this level and breadth of personal data. Yet this information can now be laid bare to government agencies, through legal backdoors and precedent. The consequences of this are potentially profound, and indeed profoundly bad for anyone who cares about privacy.

DIEM OPPOSITION

Consequently, there is already huge scepticism regarding the motivation of Facebook for entering into this sphere, and there is no doubt that many hardcore cryptocurrency users will boycott the Diem project. It would therefore be easy to make this chapter into a polemical rant on the problems associated with Facebook and its Diem coin. But let's attempt to look at the other side of the argument.

It's firstly notable that the enthusiasm of Facebook for cryptocurrency is definitely a positive for the industry.

Having one of the world's most visible and successful companies align themselves so publicly with the blockchain is unquestionably indicative of the credibility of the niche, regardless of the company's motives. Even a few years ago, it would have been unthinkable for one of the biggest corporations on the planet to launch its own cryptocurrency; now it's on the verge of occurring. Even the most vicious critic of the Diem currency would have to agree that this is a huge achievement for the Crypto and Blockchain space.

In response to privacy and data concerns, Facebook has obviously put information into the public domain already. The company has argued that information security will be one of the main priorities of the Diem project, with a system being put in place to ensure compliance with relevant laws and regulations. The integrated protection measures that will form part of the Diem coin from day one will ensure that individuals and businesses can trust its security and integrity. According to Facebook!

LOGISTICAL NIGHTMARE

As the company attempts to reassure users, Facebook has outlined how Diem will safeguard valuable information, and attempt to provide a solution that can be used by the one-billion people worldwide who currently have no access to a bank account. However, this is a huge logistical undertaking for Facebook, if it is to remotely approach the satisfaction of its privacy proclamations, and also its legal requirements.

Diem will firstly be challenged by the fact that different geographical regions have completely different laws related to cryptocurrency. The Facebook project is deemed to be very much global in nature, while also being a mainstream payment system, and this will require an intricate legal balancing act. Cynics would simply say that the privacy ethos of the project will go out of the window almost immediately!

Furthermore, it is intended for Diem to become a viable currency for eCommerce, which is going to create a vast amount of online data. The reality is that the possibility of misusing this information for either commercial or political purposes will be extremely tempting. Financial companies, retailers, governments, and any number of other interested parties would love to get hold of this data for tailored marketing and other reasons. And delivering this information is, indeed, exactly what Facebook has done historically!

Those working within Facebook to develop Diem have attempted to reassure its potential users that everything associated with the project is safe and secure. David Marcus, co-creator and a board member of Diem, spoke publicly on the subject of Facebook's crypto, and its Novi wallet, in an effort to address privacy concerns. "Basically, the way that we've designed this– and it actually took us a lot of effort to build it the right way– is that your financial data is not going to be commingled with your social data," Marcus told Yahoo Finance.[6] Marcus went on to explain that Facebook intends to disrupt the overseas retail remittance market with its cryptocurrency product, and that he believes that initial scepticism will begin to dissipate once Diem establishes itself.

Facebook certainly has the budget and marketing clout in order to achieve this, and also to make a massive splash in the cryptocurrency space. And there have been voices in the industry that argue that the Diem digital currency can revolutionize the global payment system. Enough is known about the Diem blockchain and Novi wallet to deduce that the project has a reliable technological foundation, a sophisticated standalone wallet, and an extremely well-backed coin. There are some strong principles underpinning the project, and Diem has huge potential to facilitate cross-border payments and international transactions.

DOUBTS REMAIN

However, this will do little to reassure the doubters. It is notable that early predictions related to Diem suggest that the Novi wallet will support full integration with WhatsApp, Messenger, Instagram, and probably several other platforms. This will potentially make the platform user-friendly, but it also creates a hugely interconnected system that would be ripe for data mining.

This would be troubling enough in itself, if Facebook had an unblemished record on privacy. Unfortunately, stating that Facebook hasn't exactly been perfect in this department is rather akin to suggesting that Adolf Hitler had a somewhat checkered record when it came to international relations!

It is reasonable to assert that Facebook's practices have been little short of diabolical when it comes to user privacy. The social media network has a history of highly questionable and ethically dubious conduct, so much so that the United States House Committee on Financial Services required Facebook to delay the launch of Diem until risk assessments can be properly conducted. Even when these security concerns have been addressed by the government, this will be unlikely to satisfy many market observers who will recall only too clearly precisely what Facebook has done previously.

Exhaustively documenting the extent of privacy abuses and concerns associated with Facebook is beyond the scope of this chapter. We would be here until the end of time! But it's important to outline some of the worst excesses of this corporation that has frequently been described as intrusive, monopolistic and duplicitous.

Firstly, Facebook has already paid the largest ever fine related to privacy breaches. In July, 2019, the US Federal Trade Commission (FTC) forced the social media giant to pay $5 billion in response to privacy concerns. The company was also forced to establish an independent privacy committee, over which the chief executive of Facebook, Mark Zuckerberg, will exercise no control or influence.[7]

This massive fine was in response to the allegations that political consultancy Cambridge Analytica improperly obtained the data of 87 million Facebook users. But as the investigation unfolded, its scope widened to include other issues such as facial recognition. "Despite repeated promises to its billions of users worldwide that they could control how their personal information is shared, Facebook undermined consumers' choices," FTC chairman Joe Simons commented at the time.

Another example of the lackadaisical attitude that Facebook has demonstrated with regard to user privacy came in February, 2021, when it emerged that the company was being sued for losing control of the data of over 1 million Facebook users in England and Wales. Facebook continues to oppose this action, brought by journalist Peter Jukes,[8] but its ability to legally defend its record on data privacy has been rather unsuccessful previously.

TIP OF THE ICEBERG

Indeed, the Cambridge Analytica 'crisis' is really only the tip of the iceberg. Other advertising agencies associated with Facebook have implemented similar psychological targeting for many years, and the social media behemoth even patented technology of a similar nature back in 2012.[9] The only reason that this particularly came to light was that Cambridge Analytica was so open about its methods and the caliber of clients that it had managed to attract. Eventually, the authorities sat up and paid attention. It's therefore doubtful whether even if the vast fines that Facebook have paid will dissuade the company from pursuing a similar approach in the future, whatever contrary protestations and affirmations its phalanx of executives might make.

In a sense, the fact that Facebook has chosen to acknowledge these privacy and security factors associated with Diem so publicly, even before the project has launched, is actually a damning indictment of its current position. The company knows that it has a huge credibility gap when it comes to privacy and security, and that the success, or otherwise, of Diem is almost entirely predicated on convincing people this ethos has significantly shifted. This certainly won't be an easy proposition within the cryptocurrency community, as comment sections and forums are already positively bursting with opprobrium and hostility towards Facebook.

The reality is that Facebook could easily misuse the data that is accumulated by its Diem project, that this information will be plugged into multiple sources, and that it is readily accessible to external agencies and actors due to existing legislation. Facebook cannot reasonably deny this, all the company can say publicly is that they have considered this issue really carefully, and put stringent measures in place. Ultimately, this is just hot air! Massive multinational corporations make all manner of claims that they know to be completely false and misleading every day; there is very little reason to believe that this is any different.

Diem could lead to a lot of good happening in the cryptocurrency space. It could result in the blockchain and cryptocurrencies going truly mainstream. It could familiarize billions of people with cryptocurrency, who would otherwise be very late adopters. And it could even, ironically, open people's eyes to the importance of privacy in this space.

But regardless of the potential positives, there is no doubt that Facebook faces massive challenges in bridging the credibility gap in this area, and this may be a chasm that is too great even for a company of its extraordinary resources and success. The world of cryptocurrency moves fast, and even during the period that this book was being written, five Democratic senators wrote to Zuckerberg urging him to shelve the company's digital currency plans. Whatever designs Facebook has on this space may yet be thwarted.[10]

References

1. Constantino, T. (2021). Why Amazon Will Likely Make a Massive Move Into Crypto. *Inc.*
2. Collins, B. (2021). Is Apple About To Accept Cryptocurrency? Job Ad Suggests It Might. *Forbes.*
3. Bradshaw, T. (2021). Apple ad for 'alternative payments' job signals cryptocurrency interest. *Financial Times.*
4. Johnson, C. (2020). Google Goes Blockchain? New Deal Opens A Door To Crypto. *Forbes.*
5. Zheng, S. (2019). Facebook Libra will be made up of U.S. dollar, euro, yen, pound, and Singapore dollar. *Yahoo!.*
6. *Yahoo! Finance.* (2021). How Facebook plans to 'earn people's trust' with its Novi digital wallet.
7. Carrie, J. (2019). Facebook to be fined $5bn for Cambridge Analytica privacy violations. *The Guardian.*

8. *BBC*. (2021). Facebook sued for 'losing control' of users' data.
9. Cellan-Jones, R. (2018). Facebook explored unpicking personalities to target ads. *BBC*.
10. Singh, K. (2021). U.S. lawmakers say Facebook cannot be trusted to manage cryptocurrency. *Reuters*.

CHAPTER 8
A NEW BLOCKCHAIN-BASED INFRASTRUCTURE FOR SOCIAL MEDIA

ON 4TH OCTOBER, 2021, the social network Facebook suffered a global crash. The main Facebook social media site was completely inaccessible for around seven hours, along with subsidiary sites such as Instagram, WhatsApp, Mapillary, and Oculus. The outage was little short of a disaster for Facebook, with billions of users worldwide decrying the vulnerability of its software. Ironically, during this already infamous Facebook crash, many of its users flocked to platforms such as Twitter, Discord, Snapchat, and other social media systems, which then resulted in disruptions on their servers!

The reason for the Facebook outage is quite technical and complex, but the foundation of it and its consequences are much easier to understand. Not only were Facebook users impacted by the crisis, but it even negatively affected Facebook's internal communications, preventing employees from sending and receiving emails, accessing the corporate directory and contacting colleagues, and even authenticating some internal documents and services.

Make no mistake - this was a big deal! In many ways, this connectivity issue underlines the extent to which we have become dependent on the Internet and Internet services. Some people, myself included, can remember a time when the Internet didn't exist, and we were still able to function in something approaching a coherent fashion! This is no longer possible. It's not only hard to imagine a world without the Internet, it is, in fact, hard to argue against the notion that we have become so reliant on the web that if it crashed for a significant period of time then the socio-economic consequences would be barely imaginable. How can you argue otherwise when a simple crash of Facebook, which lasted for a few hours, caused untold chaos!

INFRASTRUCTURE ISSUES

In response to the outage, Facebook issued a statement attempting to paper over the cracks of what was undoubtedly an embarrassing incident:

> "To all the people and businesses around the world who depend on us, we are sorry for the inconvenience caused by

today's outage across our platforms...People and businesses around the world rely on us every day to stay connected. We understand the impact that outages like these have on people's lives, as well as our responsibility to keep people informed about disruptions to our services. We apologize to all those affected, and we're working to understand more about what happened today so we can continue to make our infrastructure more resilient."

FACEBOOK

Beneath the usual corporate PR, there was something particularly significant in this statement. Facebook was acknowledging that its infrastructure was fundamentally vulnerable. Conceding such a failing as this is certainly not something that large companies relish doing, and particularly not publicly. But the severity of this particular issue meant that Facebook had to demonstrate that it was taking steps to improve its overall operation, in an attempt to buttress faith in its platform.

There is no doubt that the infrastructure of Facebook is hugely significant. It would be quite possible to write a book purely on the social, economic and political impact of Facebook; and indeed people have done so! Facebook has created an indelible impression on all of our lives. Even if we don't directly engage with Facebook and its related services, the advertising and even political power of Facebook is such that it has directly impacted on your life; whether you like it or not!

What is significant about Facebook is that it is based on an entirely centralized infrastructural model. As opposed to the blockchain, the users of Facebook play no part in the operation or maintenance of its network. It is stored centrally, run centrally, and, essentially, a small elite of people benefit from its success and profitability.

ATTENTION AS CAPITAL

Of course, this is perfectly normal in a capitalist model, but what is different with Facebook and other similar social media platforms is that they use the personal information of their users as a form of currency or capital. This can't really be debated. It's not something that Facebook particularly wishes to focus attention on, but the reality of its business model is undeniable.

This model has been discussed extensively in public fora, and this led to the infamous tweet from Jake Tapper: "Don't make the mistake of thinking you're Facebook's customer, you're not – you're the product. Its customers are the advertisers." This has since been repeated by many people, and a somewhat sophisticated reading of Facebook would suggest that the people who use it on a daily basis are actually the product of the website, rather than anything that the company produces itself.

There are arguments for and against this, but it is perhaps more accurate to state that the most valuable commodity for Facebook, and the entity that is ultimately its product, is not its users, but the attention of its users. This is nothing particularly new. Television, in particular, has operated in this model since its inception, delivering audiences in neatly-packaged demographics to advertisers. Indeed, it could be reasonably argued that one of the reasons that television is so vanilla in nature is that it must keep the corporations happy at all times. Television executives, especially in the United States, don't like taking risks. They don't like upsetting people. They're much happier delivering rather safe and anodyne entertainment, which ticks certain boxes, and keeps their billion-dollar clients happy.

The big difference with social media is that it cultivates highly targeted advertising. It attempts to draw your attention to aspects and items of the culture that it has deduced will specifically interest you. While television creates a generic experience, Facebook is customized to attract your eyeballs, and, arguably, to manipulate your perspective. You might see an advert for Coca-Cola on television, but you may absolutely despise this product, in which case it will have no significant impact on you. Conversely, social media can ensure that you see products, adverts, and promotions that are tailored to your interests and preferences, based on the vast amount of data that Facebook collects on all of its users.

THE DATA GAME

This information can be categorized as personal data - based on identifiable information such as phone numbers, email addresses and gender; engagement and behavioral data - which outlines how you interact with a website or application; and attitudinal data - based on the importance that you place on certain products or services. Once you have commingled all of this information, based on someone's surfing history, you gain a pretty significant insight into their overall personality and preferences.

Once you have this picture, you can then use it in several ways. For example, you can utilize the information to ensure the people become addicted to a certain platform. Facebook is certainly not the only company that attempts to do this; this is just a fundamental part of contemporary culture. You will encounter this on YouTube, Netflix, Amazon, and virtually any entertainment-based media platform. But if Facebook can keep you on its platform, it can tell advertisers that its customers spend a long time on the website, and consequently it can attract more advertising revenue.

The information can also be used in an initiative that has been referred to as 'surveillance capitalism'. One aspect of this is the targeted advertisements that have been discussed previously, but your personal data can also be sold to third parties. One of the interesting aspects of this area is that as the material that you see is customized according to your preferences, you effectively have your own position confirmed to yourself. You experience the illusion that your particular perspective is the only legitimate viewpoint, and the media that you consume completely reflects this without any dissent. You can even interact with groups solely compromised of people who agree with you! This is one of the reasons why Internet echo chambers have emerged, and why some truly alarming incidents have occurred, thanks to unregulated platforms such as 4Chan.

However, perhaps the most sinister of all is that the information that Facebook holds on you can be used to manipulate your behavior. We discussed this in the previous chapter, but the extent of this phenomenon online is gigantic. The Internet now has a much bigger influence over the opinions and culture of the human race than television. This is because the Internet is far more efficient as an opinion-former. It is instant. It can be tailored to the individual in an incredibly sophisticated way. It is much harder to censor or legislate against. Its audience is much bigger than television, as you can connect with anyone on the planet immediately. Consequently, the cultural impact of the Internet has become almost incalculable, and although social media doesn't completely dominate the contemporary web, it certainly wields an enormous influence over the discourse in cyberspace.

BIGGEST AUDIENCE EVER

This is all already hugely significant. But it's going to become even more significant in the future. The global annual market size of social media is currently around $94 billion, but this is set to grow exponentially over the next few years, exceeding $300 billion by 2025. By this time, 4.5 billion people will be using social media on a regular basis; over half of the world's population.[1] There has never been any form of media in the entirety of human history that has achieved this level of penetration. The seriousness of this simply cannot be overstated.

Before we move on to discussing the importance of the blockchain in this area, I would briefly like to point out the counter-arguments to the previous discussion in this chapter. Ultimately, we all have freedom of choice. It is true that social media platforms wage what are pretty sophisticated campaigns against the general public (and I don't think it's too strong to say 'against'). But that's just part of modern life; it's nothing new; it's simply more advanced and technologically-driven than has been possible previously.

Ultimately, if you want to take control of your own mind in this or any other culture, you have a responsibility to never accept anything that you read at face value. Don't take my word for anything that is written in this book; look it up for yourself. That should be our guiding principle. We should all actively seek out both sides of every argument, and all possible perspectives, before we form our opinions. Now I fully accept that most people won't do this, but that is what is required in order to be informed, or at least to have a chance of being informed. And if you're not willing to do it, you will be prone to manipulation. That is true regardless of the existence of Facebook, or any other platform.

FREE VERSUS FREEDOM

Where the blockchain comes into this issue is that it offers a potentially decentralized platform, in which social media operates in a completely different fashion. In a decentralized social media model, production and running costs can be split across numerous actors. This is the case with Steemit, where the entire infrastructure is maintained by a number of independent witnesses, elected publicly and promoted or demoted by stakeholder votes. This is one of the critical things to understand about Facebook; its founders would argue that everything it does that has been criticized, often with good reason, is simply carried out in order to ensure that the website is free to its users. It will view this as an entirely reasonable argument, and it probably is a reasonable argument.

But the problem with getting something for free is that you don't value it, and you don't invest any responsibility in the platform. As Jeff Goldblum's character notes in Jurassic Park about the dinosaur theme park that has been created: "The problem with the scientific power that you're using here...it didn't require any discipline to attain it. You read what others had done and you took the next step. You didn't earn the knowledge for yourselves, so you don't take any responsibility for it." And this has been very true of Facebook as a platform. Unquestionably, people have posted things on Facebook that they would have been much more cautious about on a paid platform, and certainly a work-related platform. The fact that it is free and so easily accessible leads to a rather flippant attitude, whereby people feel that they don't need to understand the underlying issues relating to Facebook, or the consequences of them.

Equally, the small elite that runs and benefits from Facebook is so inaccessible to its users that it might as well not exist. It could just as easily be a figment of our collective imagination. It is in no way accountable, and in no meaningful way can be held accountable, except by people leaving the platform. In fact, even when Facebook suffered the outage mentioned at the beginning of this chapter, which wiped $6 billion from its stock value, [2] its owner and CEO, Mark Zuckerberg, barely bothered to comment, and certainly wasn't publicly available for discussion. When Facebook recently rebranded its corporate identity as Meta, he did release a pre-recorded video, but at this time one wonders whether he'll ever allow himself to be interviewed publicly again, or caught in a non-arranged and spontaneous commenting situation! Certainly, he's not about to be deselected or voted out of existence!

THE NEW MODEL

Conversely, with decentralized social media platforms based on blockchains, witnesses receive a portion of the revenues of the platform via minted tokens. For example, one new blockchain-based platform, Steemit, stakes coins via Steem Power. The more attention that this blogging-based website attracts, the more that it is worth, and the more that coins increase in value. There is therefore an incentive to maintain the platform, as users will only be rewarded when it is functioning adequately. This is a direct involvement and transparency that completely contrasts with the Facebook model.

Equally, with a blockchain-based social media model, all participants agree on a set of rules, and then they collectively enforce them in accordance with the issuance of tokens. On Steemit, users create content that offers value to the network, which then facilitates the distribution of this currency to a larger number of users.

Centralized services are also easy to hack by their very nature. When a centralized location is used for the storage of user data, any breach of the system can naturally be disastrous - we've already discussed the failures of Facebook in this area in the previous chapter. Of course, this doesn't apply to the blockchain, which is precisely designed to deliver a level of privacy that is currently unequalled. This is why it is ideally suited to the social media niche, once the platforms that have adopted the blockchain for social media content have achieved market penetration.

Aside from Steemit, another such example of blockchain-based social media is Indorse; built on the Ethereum blockchain. Indorse is a professional network, with a similar business model to LinkedIn. The big difference with Indorse is that users earn rewards for sharing professional skills on the platform. This incentivization model will become common in blockchain-based social media, and ultimately offers motivation for people to get involved and participate both actively and responsibly.

Indeed, Indorse aims to resolve three fundamental problems of social networking platforms, namely economy, autonomy and trust. With this in mind, Indorse offers internal reward and reputation systems, ensuring that members not only cultivate and advertise their own skills and accomplishments, they also endorse other members as well.

Another example of blockchain-based social media is UTO.ONE, built on the EOSIO blockchain. This is another platform that offers tokens for members when they interact with the platform and other users in the community. Again, the focus with UTO.ONE is on privacy and security, with its blockchain-based approach eliminating bots and fake accounts via a process for verification. All actions are immutable and traceable, meaning that bullying, fraud, and illegal activity can effectively be eliminated.

DSCVR is another decentralized social content forum, which enables users to control content, and even the platform itself. Offering similar functionality to Reddit, DSCVR flips this on its head by ensuring that its community dictates the direction of the site through a tokenized framework. DSCVR has amassed 14,000 users since it launched in June. And Distrikt is a LinkedIn alternative, showcasing professional qualifications and credentials, while being entirely blockchain-based. Both of these sites also allow easy access, with users able to log in via biometrics, such as fingerprint recognition.

This all sounds exciting, but one particular initiative of Steemit is particularly enticing. The objective of this platform is to develop an algorithm that can evaluate individual contributions based on a reasonable estimate of their subjective worth to the community. Within this idealized system, members of the community will work together, assessing one another as contributors and determining what would be fair reward for their work. In order to achieve this, Steemit is working towards developing algorithms that are resistant to profit-driven manipulation, delivering a fair system that is based on sound economics. This would be the ultimate achievement; creating a social media platform that not only encourages responsibility, but that is also effectively a meritocracy.

EARLY DAYS

It's definitely early days for blockchain-based social media, and it's not realistic to expect the number of users on these platforms that are associated with Facebook and other big names. There are always barriers to entry in any major industry, and the likes of Steemit and Indorse will need to demonstrate that they can match the level of user experience offered by existing platforms and applications.

However, aside from the qualities associated with these new forms of media, platforms can also incentivize users to switch. Free tokens and NFTs can be used to encourage people to sign up. And as the privacy aspect of social media becomes an increasingly prominent issue, there is definitely potential for blockchain equivalents to grow.

It's clear that the blockchain-based social platforms emerging now embody an ethos that Facebook and other social media giants have been unable to deliver, and one that could seriously disrupt this space.

References

1. *Statista*. (2020). Number of social network users worldwide from 2017 to 2025.
2. *Evening Standard*. (2021). Mark Zuckerberg's net worth dives $6 billion after Facebook stock crashes on outage

CHAPTER 9
MOBILE PHONES AND BLOCKCHAIN

SMARTPHONES ALREADY PLAY a critical role in our lives, with considerable evidence indicating that they have become not only the dominant mobile platform, but, in fact, the pre-eminent computing platform. For example, Statista data indicates that 85% of Americans currently have mobile phones,[1] with this figure also being reflected globally in the over 80% of people that own mobile phones worldwide.[2] The growth is far from being limited to the Western world either; the China Internet Network Information Center research found that 99.3% of all internet users in China go online via their mobile devices.[3]

This is significant, as in many ways mobile phone platforms are the ideal companion for the blockchain. This is particularly true with 5G on the horizon, which will deliver a faster, more secure user experience. Meanwhile, dApps will open up an entirely new ecosystem for the space. Mobile infrastructure will be critical in the future development of technology, and, in turn, the blockchain. Indeed, we have been hearing about the development of 5G and even 6G for quite some time. Yet many of us remain in the dark regarding how it will actually impact our lives, or even how it will influence the way that we interact with our mobile technology.

WEB 3.0

One concept that is critical in the answer to this question is the Semantic Web - far more commonly referred to as Web 3.0. In simple terms, this is an extension of the existing Internet, with the underlying aim of ensuring that Internet data is readable by machines. The inventor of the Internet, Tim Berners-Lee, had imagined an intelligent World Wide Web way back in 1999, and it seems that his original vision is finally on the horizon.

There are many potential consequences of this technological development, but one of the most significant is the increasing decentralization of infrastructure. It is unarguable that the Internet has had the greatest social and commercial impact of any technological phenomenon in recent decades. Of course, the blockchain itself simply wouldn't exist without the Internet to support it.

But a major problem with what is referred to as Web 2.0 - essentially, the existing Internet infrastructure - is its reliance on centralization. We have discussed many of the facets of this in previous chapters, but the consequences of this centralization have included negative elements. Inevitably, as the Internet has matured, some undesirable aspects related to it have emerged, with snooping, surveillance, exploitative advertising, and intrusive user targeting just some of the commonly encountered issues.

With Web 3.0, decentralized infrastructure and application platforms will displace the centralized tech giants, handing individuals the opportunity to claim rightful control over their own data. As we've established, this has been a massive problem across the existing Internet infrastructure, particularly with social media giants such as Facebook.

ORIGINAL ETHOS

When the Internet was originally envisaged and created, there was certainly no intention for it to be dominated by massive corporations, who would then profiteer off the general public. That was a country mile away from the original ethos of the concept, which was to democratize access to information. In accordance with this, Web 3.0 promises to deliver transparent, opt-in, peer-to-peer communications that hand control over information back to users.

But there are other important aspects to Web 3.0. One of the most critical is that augmented reality and virtual reality are expected to be primary gateways for access to this platform. There has been a huge amount of investment in this area, and the first truly successful virtual reality products are now available on the market.

It is interesting that Facebook has been an active participant in this area, having completed the $2 billion acquisition of Oculus VR in 2014, while its 'Meta' rebranding and 'Metaverse' concept are centered on the importance of virtual reality in this new Internet system. While we should remain vigilant regarding Facebook, and sceptical to a certain extent, its emphasis on this new direction for the web is hugely significant.

The potential of Web 3.0 could be discussed at great length, but what significance does this have for the blockchain? The important thing to understand is that the quantity and diversity of data is increasing massively now, and this will only accelerate as the number of active Internet devices, associated with the Internet of Things, inevitably proliferate. While many people are excited about Internet of Things technology and its potential, there is also no doubt that privacy is a critical consideration with this emerging system.

But this is where blockchain comes in. All of the technologies that are already associated with the fully operable digital ledgers used by blockchains will be hugely advantageous when this new form of the Internet emerges. Blockchain will be practically foundational with Web 3.0, enabling the system to be operated without having to impose onerous restrictions on users.

THE HEALTHCARE SYSTEM OF THE FUTURE

It can be tricky to comprehend or imagine what Web 3.0 will look like, let alone its advantages over the existing Internet. So here is an example from the healthcare system of the future.

Suddenly, immense connectivity, processing power, digital devices, data analysis and comprehension, and virtual reality applications have commingled to create entirely new capabilities for healthcare professionals. In this new world, we no longer interact with digital information through the crude interface of traditional screens; everything has been opened up into an augmented and virtual reality world.

Instead of interfacing with traditional data, a heart surgeon simply initiates his or her hands-free intelligent device, and receives curated data across multiple media channels. These all appear within the field of view, as we've seen represented in countless science-fiction movies over the years, such as Avatar. She can then interact with this data, even utilizing her intelligent device to arrange virtual meetings with other important healthcare professionals.

As one of the world's leading cardiovascular experts, this doctor no longer needs to be in the vicinity of a patient. Instead, it is now possible to digitally sign into robotic surgery on people located thousands of miles away. This involves guiding on-site human and robotic colleagues in the physical operating room, administering procedures using haptic-enabled and custom 3D-printed surgical instruments, alongside hands-free digital models.

Before the process even begins, everyone involved with the operation holds a virtual conference, in which they collectively explore a 3D digital model of the patient's heart. This is an exact digital replica, and makes it possible for the surgeons to decide upon a plan of action. And once the operation is completed, this multifaceted system automatically collects, organizes and analyses data, while also intelligently dealing with security permissions.

That's really only scratching the surface of possibility in the healthcare sector, which is, of course, only one industry. But a considerably more joined-up, intelligent, flexible future is looming into view; it is actually not that far ahead on the horizon. Unless you are, with respect, quite old then this will happen in your lifetime! Already, there are Internet connected networks of healthcare systems, millions of digital patient consultations occur every year, and even some of the more advanced virtual reality, AI and robotics functionality is already possible. Web 3.0 and the blockchain will play a major role in integrating and managing these advanced technologies, ensuring that they can interact securely.

EVOLVING HUMAN CULTURE

This system is definitely not ready to go live yet. The mass deployment of 5G has yet to occur, and it could be several years until this arrives; let alone 6G! When this new mobile infrastructure is in place, the hugely improved speed that mobile networks will benefit from will increase reliability and functionality, leading to a new wave of technologies that underpins an evolving human culture. There are even examples of this new approach to Internet connectivity emerging now; for example, a company that is literally named Spatial raised $14 million to build a holographic 3D workspace application.[4] What seemed like science-fiction is already becoming science fact.

Another advantage of the decentralized Web 3.0 infrastructure is a significantly reduced risk of downtime. Web 3.0 servers and dApps would be run on, for example, Ethereum's decentralized network of tens of thousands of computers. This would also greatly reduce the efficacy of DDoS attacks and other nefarious activity aimed at servers, inherently improving the reliability of the system. As there is no single point of failure, the network will be able to function as normal regardless of participants being attacked or eliminated.

It should also be mentioned that Web 3.0 faces challenges, as is almost inevitably the case with the adoption of any major innovation. It's worth remembering that while the Internet has been a categorical success, it wasn't adopted overnight, particularly at the domestic level. Hard though it may be to believe, there were only 361 million regular Internet users at the turn of the century.[5] Equally, although the advantages of Web 3.0 are already understood, and its possibilities are being explored, it will take some time to replace the existing infrastructure.

One of the major issues that must be addressed is the speed of the decentralized web in comparison to the existing Internet. At the time of writing, the need for authentication nodes with Web 3.0 technology means that the decentralized web is slower than Web 2.0. This can change over time as technology develops and evolves, but it's going to be difficult to convince people to switch until Web 3.0 delivers comparable speeds to the current infrastructure.

Scalability is also considered an ongoing issue. With the existing architecture imagined for Web 3.0, every transaction must be processed by all nodes. This can lead to network congestion, limiting the ability of the blockchain to handle enterprise-class applications. Again, this is a critical question of functionality, as people will not switch to Web 3.0 until it can deliver the quality of software and features that we all take for granted today. This is one area where competing blockchains could be a major advantage. Ethereum is being developed to deal with this right now, but other solutions, such as Cardano and Polkadot, could also supersede Ethereum.

Nonetheless, while issues such as latency, scale and reliability represent challenges in transition, there are a wealth of organizations focused on delivering a new Internet model. As the adoption of this new standard rises, the network effect will begin to multiply the benefits of Web 3.0, leading to more users jumping ship. It is not a transition that will happen rapidly, but it will occur inexorably, as the model associated with Web 2.0 becomes increasingly dated, moribund and even obsolete.

BLOCKCHAIN PHONES

Web 3.0 access will remain limited until dApps roll out en masse. But you can actually purchase a blockchain phone right now! HTC has already announced an Exodus S1 blockchain phone, alongside several other handsets. The electronics manufacturer has even collaborated with the Binance exchange to deliver a special limited edition of the smartphone.

But what is actually offered by a blockchain phone? This is very much dependent on the individual device, but, fundamentally, each blockchain phone is designed to place a stronger emphasis on blockchain, crypto, and decentralized applications. This is certainly not the case with existing iOS and Android handsets, which are built with the existing Internet infrastructure in mind. There is absolutely nothing preventing Apple or Google from delivering technology aligned with Web 3.0, but there will be far greater plurality and freedom in the market.

HTC evidently sees an opportunity in the Web 3.0 and blockchain niche, and has consequently already delivered several blockchain phones. The Exodus 1S is a more affordable version of the Exodus, delivering the sort of specs associated with high-end smartphones. Its Quad HD+ display, Snapdragon 845 chip, dual-camera setup and 3,500mAh battery pack means that it competes effectively with more traditional smartphones.

However, even Samsung's flagship S22 phone is more blockchain-friendly than previous releases. The latest iteration of this hugely successful series of mobile products makes it possible for users to manage and trade virtual assets from third-party wallets. Support for hardware wallets provides the Galaxy blockchain with a consistent user experience of managing crypto assets from one convenient location, while users can also connect to hardware wallets, including the Ledger Nano S and Ledger Nano X.

Samsung is keen to emphasize that its proprietary Samsung Blockchain Wallet is also compatible with a range of the most popular cryptocurrencies, including Bitcoin, Ethereum, Tron and ERC tokens. There is also support for dApps, with the Korean manufacturer even offering users recommendations across a variety of categories. There is also an iOS wallet, although the notoriously restrictive Apple has been a little less enthusiastic about publicly advocating blockchain technology.

LESSER KNOWN MANUFACTURERS

However, aside from the big names in the smartphone market, some lesser known manufacturers are also making an impression with smartphone technology focused on the blockchain. The Sirin Labs Finney features a distinctive sloping design, and touts itself as being a "state-of-the-art ultra-secured Blockchain smartphone". Meanwhile, the Pundi XPhone combines its blockchain compatibility with modular qualities, meaning that you can combine various attachments within one device.

At the moment, blockchain phones can be considered quite niche. But their designated ability to handle all aspects of the burgeoning Web 3.0, most importantly accessing decentralized apps and social networks, will be critical going forward. They also offer a level of security that can never be achieved by a conventional smartphone.

In fact, most savvy market observers believe that blockchain on smartphone platforms should be considered self-evidently viable. Eventually, all smartphones will be enriched with blockchain capabilities and wallets, particularly as Bitcoin and Ethereum become ever more mainstream. These innovative products will even help users share bandwidth via peer-to-peer blockchains, in the process helping to address mobile data issues.

An interesting initiative in this area is the formation of the World Mobile organization, which is being informed and directed by several veterans of the VoIP industry. The intention of World Mobile is to become the first "blockchain-powered mobile operator", delivering its own blockchain, operating system, and network architecture. This would then offer users decentralized mobile access all over the world, with an emphasis on data privacy and security.

NUMEROUS ADVANTAGES

The new blockchain-enabled smartphone infrastructure promises numerous advantages over existing mobile architecture. But one of the most obvious is that users will be part of a completely different ecosystem, which is not controlled by the giants of Apple and Google. There will be far more variety in terms of providers in this space, and it will be much more difficult for megacorporations to dominate and control the way that the market evolves. We will see Android and even iPhone devices that fully embrace the blockchain, but it won't be as necessary for users to rely on them. And as privacy becomes an ever more important issue, Apple and Google will actually have to deliver in this area, or face the threat of being increasingly excluded by concerned and principled consumers.

Another advantage of blockchain phones is that logging into applications will be far easier, with usernames and passwords no longer required. A blockchain phone will deliver an intelligent system, in which user information is both more secure and customized for individual preference. The boundaries of what is possible with both smartphones and the Internet will open up massively, with functionality that can barely be imagined today becoming a reality.

Web 3.0 won't be available for mass adoption immediately. The development of this new Internet infrastructure will take some time. But the evolution of blockchain technology is moving rapidly. Investment in this space is huge. Make no mistake - Web 3.0 is coming. It will be here soon. And when it does arrive, it is going to change people's lives in a way that is both exciting and beneficial. This is the next great quantum leap in human culture and society.

References

1. O. Dea, S. (2021). Smartphones in the U.S. - Statistics & Facts. *Statisa*.
2. *BankMyCell*. (2021). November 2021 Mobile User Statistics: Discover the Number of Phones in The World & Smartphone Penetration by Country or Region.
3. Shen, X. (2020). China now has over 900 million internet users thanks to the pandemic. *South China Morning Post*.
4. Lunden, I. (2020). Spatial raises $14M more for a holographic 3D workspace app, a VR/AR version of Zoom or Hangouts. *TechCrunch*.
5. *Pingdom*. (2010). The incredible growth of the Internet since 2000.

CHAPTER 10
THE INTERNET AND WEB 3.0 - THE NEW DECENTRALIZED INTERNET FOR EVERYONE - IT'S ALREADY HERE

WE'VE NOW ESTABLISHED that Web 3.0 is on the horizon. But how did we get here?

The Internet has evolved over a period of time, and this new iteration of the World Wide Web is simply a natural successor in this sequential process. The original Internet emerged thanks to a project launched by the Defense Advanced Research Projects Agency (DARPA). The whole concept of the Internet was to build a global network that enhanced digital communications. Even many pioneers of the web could not have envisaged at that time what it would become. Its evolution has exceeded even the perception of the visionaries that created it.

Web 1.0 was the result of this early research and development, and this system was relatively simplistic compared to the contemporary Internet. The early web was essentially comprised of interconnected webpages, joined by hyperlinks. There was none of the additional functionality and control that is possible today, and it is thus often referred to as the 'read-only Internet'. The level of interactivity associated with Web 1.0 was significantly diminished. Information was disseminated, but there was virtually no communication between users of the Internet. There was also absolutely no advertising!

THE ADVENT OF WEB 2.0

As the Internet grew in popularity, and more people realized that it could be a useful and entertaining platform, the need for enhanced technology became obvious. Static pages could provide valuable information, but to reach the next level the Internet had to evolve. This process of evolution eventually resulted in the Internet that we witness today, which is often described as Web 2.0. But, in reality, there was no cast-iron transition point where Web 1.0 became Web 2.0. This occurred over a period of time as new technologies became available, and the Internet slowly but surely became something new and considerably more dynamic.

There are many aspects to the contemporary Internet that we take for granted, and these include complex visual material, real-time video, and all manner of interactive platforms. Today, it's possible to conduct virtually all social and economic activity via the Internet, which is both hugely advantageous, and also potentially dangerous in certain circumstances. While the Internet has undoubtedly been a major positive, it can also contribute to a culture that it is increasingly atomized and reclusive. There is no easy answer to this issue, but the very fact that so much can be achieved without ever leaving your house can be deleterious for those inclined towards agoraphobia and other similar disorders.

Nonetheless, Web 2.0 has opened up a world of opportunity. And it's only by comparing and contrasting this new Internet with its forerunner that we can see how much it has evolved.

For example, Web 1.0 did feature e-commerce and online retail. But it was greatly simplified compared to what you would expect from shopping online today. An e-commerce store on Web 1.0 would be little more than a catalogue via which users could view products and services. Some early e-commerce stores wouldn't even have a shopping cart system, and would instead require users to email the proprietor to order products. It's hard to imagine Amazon becoming so powerful and successful with such a system; not quite as convenient as '1-click' ordering! Conversely, today we have e-commerce stores that are hugely sophisticated, built to accommodate automatic credit card payments, with all manner of interactivity and complex transactions possible.

INTERACTION AND COMMUNICATION

Probably the most significant aspect of Web 2.0 is the participatory nature of the system. The Internet has become an immense platform for people to communicate, and this is achieved via an almost innumerable variety of platforms. The emphasis is now on user-generated content and access, with an interoperability with other products that means the Internet is hugely flexible for end users. It's now very difficult to imagine the world without social media, and this phenomenon has unquestionably had a huge impact on our culture. Yet Twitter and Facebook would have been completely impossible with Web 1.0; the technology simply didn't support such interactivity.

The original Internet curator, Tim Berners-Lee, did envisage the web to be "a collaborative medium, a place where we [could] all meet and read and write".[1] But this only became achievable by advancements in technology that have occurred over the last couple of decades. This has helped to create an Internet culture that is peppered with communities and niche interests, where people utilize creativity and collaborate with others located all over the world.

In this respect, Web 2.0 has become an incredible tool for communication and creation. Possibly the most important lesson of Web 2.0 is that users add value to any system. Thus, newspapers encourage commenters, online retail websites encourage reviews, and virtually every platform seeks to actively involve its audience in its everyday functioning. This can be contrasted with traditional newspapers, for example, which involved minimal interactivity with readers - perhaps a letters page would be the only example - and certainly not in real-time.

COMMUNITY CULTURE

This is one of the primary reasons that cryptocurrency and blockchain have been so successful in the Internet era. Both the people that launched the early cryptocurrencies and their communities intrinsically understood the ethos behind them. They were products of a community-led culture, in which everyone contributes to the system, and the system is enhanced as a result. Again, this can be contrasted with traditional commerce and finance, in which banks traditionally advertise themselves as the custodians of the interests of customers. It's actually intriguing to view banking commercials nowadays, as even the world's most successful financial institutions have accepted that they need to be less stuffy and more inclusive. There is now far more emphasis placed on listening to customers and delivering customized services that meet the needs of patrons, rather than cramming customers into restrictive products (even if this often merely represents PR). This certainly wasn't always the case - the emphasis with bank adverts of the 1980s would be on conveying to the customer that the bank had existed for many years, they were experts, they knew what they were doing, so trust them and shut up!

Ultimately, the modern Internet has developed, both deliberately and inadvertently, a culture and architecture of participation. An essential part of the contemporary Internet is harnessing collective intelligence and abilities, creating a web that represents a globalized brain of all users' skills, thoughts, imagination and opinions. This can be negative at times; it's not for nothing that the Internet has spawned the term 'hive mind'. But, overwhelmingly, it has been positive for both culture and society, bringing people closer together, and fostering a genuinely globalized culture, in which people have a greater appreciation of aspects of the world that are external to their immediate bubble.

Everyone has access to everything nowadays, and this has led to a considerably more informed populace. While misinformation remains an issue with the Internet, it can be said conversely that no one has any reason to be uninformed today. Discernment is required, but all information can be made available to anyone, which has certainly not been the case historically. It was only possible to record information in anything approaching a sophisticated fashion with the advent of the printing press, and even then for many centuries the written word was concealed in dusty tomes, with most of the population completely illiterate.

And, of course, the Internet has created a culture of intellectual renewal. The information on the Internet is continually tweaked and reinvented, as new data becomes available. This has meant that, for example, encyclopedias have become completely obsolete. At one time, a collection of encyclopedias was the epitome of an educated mind. Today, the ownership of an encyclopedia would merely prove that you were completely out of touch, and failed to realize that the information was being superseded on an almost daily basis!

COLLABORATION TOOLS

In accordance with this participatory culture, the contemporary Internet has developed tools that feed into this architecture of collaboration and volunteerism. Open-source projects have greatly contributed to the notion of the community, with vast numbers of users contributing to some of the best-known Internet projects, such as Linux, Apache, and Perl. The success of these concepts clearly played a role in the creation of cryptocurrencies, which absolutely emanate from this culture of community contribution. Even some of the more traditional corporate success stories have been reliant on interactivity; Amazon's business model is almost entirely reliant on this facet of its operation.

However, although the Web 2.0 environment is a wonderful contributor to human society, it is still hampered by major disadvantages. The Internet is a completely open forum, but one in which anonymity is still completely normal. This means that identity theft, cybercrime, and even bullying have become commonplace. Misinformation is normal, and propaganda campaigns can spread like wildfire.

The other major issue with Web 2.0 is that its architecture is increasingly dominated by mega-corporations. Google and Facebook effectively control the contemporary Internet, and this means that two of the most profitable companies on the planet effectively control the information that you're able to access. While there has been a centralization of traditional media, it has never and can never become as centralized as the Internet. We are living in a post-Google world, in which the existence of the world's most popular search engine is almost unimaginable, and therefore it wields an extraordinary degree of power.

WEB 3.0 EMERGES

This is where Web 3.0 comes in. This new system will be built on an entirely decentralized system that will fundamentally change the way that the Internet operates. And those that are particularly enthusiastic about the Web 3.0 believe that semantic web data mapping will transform the Internet into a read, write and execute system, where automated programs enhance user experiences and contribute to the maintenance of its architecture.

We should never forget that privacy should be a fundamental human right. Yet this is something that is seriously lacking within the existing structure of the Internet. Big technology companies are constantly monitoring everything that we do, and corporations, banks and even governments are utilizing ecosystems to control everything in our lives. Often, we are little more than unwitting participants in this system, without even realizing the level of influence, and even control, that it has over our perspectives and existence.

Web 3.0 is therefore essential. It will lead to Internet usage being convenient, private and secure. And blockchain will play a major role in laying the groundwork for this transition. The existing Internet has unquestionably made a massive contribution to human society and evolution, but it equally undeniably features serious defects as well. Hacks, identity theft, data loss and privacy issues are all massive problems; illustrating this, there were 4.8 million identity theft and fraud reports received by the FTC in 2020, increasing by 45 percent from the 3.3 million reported in 2019.[2] Even the architecture itself is beginning to become creaky; unable to handle the next-level applications that are promised by Web 3.0.

DATA PRIVACY

The problems with data privacy on the existing Internet are essentially due to two factors. Firstly, the current Internet model has no intrinsic tools that enable the identification of senders of information. And, secondly, there is no native way to ensure that data hasn't been altered, copied, or manipulated during transmission. Keen advocates of the blockchain will already sense a solution to the second issue!

Currently, we rely on third parties to paper over these cracks. But, as we know from the multitude of data leaks and other hacking issues, this is far from perfect! No matter how much companies may attempt to reassure us that our data is completely safe online, the shrewd and savvy amongst us surely recognize that nothing is completely secure on the Internet. This is increasingly problematic when the information is so heavily concentrated in the hands of the few companies that control the major data platforms, especially as they haven't always done so particularly responsibly.

The blockchain will be the foundation for Web 3.0. With blockchain technology, vast groups of people are able to share important data and exchange value with complete confidence in the integrity of the information, let alone the requirement for third-party intermediaries. This is no longer a niche concept, it is something that is being explored and implemented by massive companies and even government departments.

Distributed ledger technology will bring massive value to Web 3.0, essentially fixing many of the undermining issues that exist in Web 2.0. This can be seen by the recent release of the Brave browser, which has already reached over 20 million downloads since its emergence in 2019.[3] The main objective of this software is to provide private, secure and fast browsing. Brave blocks unwanted adverts and does not collect any personal data on users. This is currently a revelation, but will be the normal model as Web 3.0 develops.

The new capabilities of Web 3.0 can be combined with the blockchain to create new online capabilities and platforms, allied to a healthier Internet culture. With Web 3.0, it will be possible to create an entirely new subset of Internet usage that can be described as self-sovereign identity. As part of this paradigm, users will maintain and control their personal data, and will no longer be reliant on third parties to secure their information online. Instead of constantly providing personal data to any and all websites, you'll instead authorize platforms to access your data as required. If any of your details change, you will simply alter this once, and then will then apply across all platforms. This technology will help create a far more trustworthy and immutable Internet than the one that exists currently, solving the delicate issues of privacy, transparency and security.

This can be combined with natural language processing provided by artificial intelligence to ensure that users receive faster, more relevant and intelligent results. This can also be massively customized to ensure that everyone is essentially surfing a different Internet. Web 3.0 will also be more connected thanks to metadata, which will evolve the whole user experience to a new level of connectivity. Content will be accessible by multiple applications, with every conceivable device connected to the Internet, meaning that services can be accessed anywhere and everywhere.

WEB TRANSITION

This transition from Web 2.0 to 3.0 is gradually taking effect, even though the average person in the street knows nothing about it whatsoever. But, as we discussed previously, this is true of almost any technological advancement. At first it seems incomprehensible, then unimaginable, then obscure, and then inevitable!

The early pioneers of the Web 3.0 concept have already emerged. One of the most successful is Steemit - the social media platform that enables people to exchange content for value. Social media is one area in which Web 3.0 will be hugely influential, not least because although the existing platforms are hugely popular, many users recognize that the business models associated with them are fundamentally broken. They don't work for the majority of users; they work only for a privileged elite.

In this regard, the Steem blockchain is a pioneering example of how creators of content can be curated by a community. The platform is completely free of adverts, while no data is either stored or sold to third parties. Content cannot be censored by a central organization, and users are awarded cryptocurrency and kudos in the community for improving the quality of Steemit content. When we consider a platform such as Steemit, suddenly a future looms into view that is based on qualitative values, as opposed to the quantitative emphasis of the contemporary Internet.

There are many other similar applications already emerging, including DTube, a YouTube alternative, and dMania, a decentralized 9GAG - a Hong Kong-based social media platform. This is only just the beginning, because as Web 3.0 evolves there will no doubt be a range of emerging technologies and solutions that completely exceed the boundaries of our existing imagination! But the most important aspect of Web 3.0 is that the emphasis will no longer be placed on the control of the platform, and ultimately information, by megacorporations. Instead, the platform will be curated and controlled by its users, as was always envisioned for the Internet by its creators.

THE REVOLUTION

The Internet has created a revolution in the way that we communicate and live our everyday lives. But it has also morphed into an insecure and sometimes intimidating platform. Blockchain and Web 3.0 will ensure that this is no longer the case, instead enabling our online existence to become more safe, secure, and even profitable.

This dizzying array of changes that are on the horizon with Web 3.0 can be challenging for our sense of conception. It's hard to imagine that the existing Internet can be replaced by an entirely different system, considering its cultural ubiquity. But, equally, it is difficult to imagine a world without the Internet at all, just as it would have been difficult for people who lived before the Internet to imagine the world that we live in now. Human progress is predicated on technological development, and the perfect storm of inventiveness and access has come together to make Web 3.0 not just a feasible reality, but quite clearly beneficial and desirable.

Web 3.0 will change our lives in many ways. Technologies will be forged that make previously impossible things seem routine. But none of these changes will be possible without the assistance of blockchain technology, which will be the backbone of this evolution of the Internet. This is one of the critical reasons that the blockchain is so important as an innovation, as it will pave the way for a new online and human culture that will be more democratized, more accessible, more advanced, and more beneficial to humanity.

Thus, it's critical for business people, entrepreneurs, developers, investors, and even just general users of the Internet to learn about the development of Web 3.0, and understand the opportunities that will be created by the decentralized technologies associated with it.

Using Web 3.0 and the blockchain to your advantage will be essential to your future prosperity.

References

1. Silver, C. (2020). What is Web 3.0?. *Forbes*.
2. *Insurance Information Institute*. (2021). Facts + Statistics: Identity theft and cybercrime.
3. *Brave*. (2020). Brave Passes 20 Million Monthly Active Users and 7 Million Daily Active Users.

CONCLUSION

When we consider the future of cryptocurrency, the whole nature of this contemplation has changed tack recently. No longer is it relevant to muse on whether cryptocurrency does indeed have a future. Its future is secure. Only the direction of cryptos, blockchains, NFTs, and all related technology and innovations remains uncertain. And also exciting!

Asserting that cryptos will completely replace traditional currency is probably too strong. Nor is a cashless society necessarily desirable. Why shouldn't a window cleaner be able to receive payment in cash, for example? But, equally, the naysayers who dismissed cryptocurrency as a passing fad and ultimate irrelevant now look about as sensible as those that were initially sceptical of e-commerce.

The open acceptance of the importance of cryptocurrency was succinctly illustrated when Eric Adams, mayor-elect for New York City, indicated his desire to receive his first three paychecks in Bitcoin. Adams also spoke of his intention to make New York the "centre of the cryptocurrency industry"; an explicit enthusiasm for cryptocurrency that can be completely contrasted with the initial pronouncements of those in positions of power and influence.

Indeed, at the time of writing, the Biden administration is laying the foundations for the regulation of cryptocurrency. This promises to be a complicated process, involving Congress, the Securities and Exchange Commission and the Commodity Futures Trading Commission. But, again, this is a clear indication that cryptocurrency is here to stay, and that major coins and tokens will play an important role in the future economy.

Aside from their economic contribution, there are practical reasons why cryptos will be part of the fabric of society going forward. One of the most compelling is that cryptocurrencies and related technology facilitate cross-border payments – delivering both efficiency and affordability – in a way that no other technology or existing system can compete with. It seems almost inevitable that blockchain and cryptos will play a major role in this important aspect of the contemporary economy, further strengthening the ties between often geographically disparate parts of the world.

And it's really blockchain technology that will be so important for this entire space as it continues to evolve. The ledger technology associated with the blockchain will offer a myriad of engaging and revolutionary possibilities across multiple industries. In fact, new ways of utilizing blockchain emerge every day. Major companies are already utilizing blockchain within their supply chains.

As the blockchain becomes increasingly prominent, the utilization of the technology will no longer be limited to the private sector. Governments are likely to begin implementing distributed ledger technology to replace existing systems. This migration is already beginning, but the blockchain will accelerate it given its qualities of immutability and privacy.

While the trust that can be associated with the blockchain will also result in greater transparency and cooperation between industries. Being able to rely on a single system across industrial strata, as opposed to operating different platforms for different industries, will play a major role in oiling the wheels of commerce and development. Blockchain will have a much bigger impact on society, and their lives, than most people currently realize.

There is also almost an entirely new world being created by NFTs and the functionality that this technology offers. Several related variables contribute to this particular equation, with the NFT tokens, related technology, the metaverse, gaming, platforms such as Twitch, and a vibrant culture driven by a generation that immediately appreciates all of this innovation all being part of the process.

It is easy to underestimate the importance of this, but that would be a grave error. EA CEO Andrew Wilson recently described NFT games that exhibit a 'play-to-earn' model as "the future of our industry". In a widely-quoted prediction for the future of gaming, Wilson commented that "in the context of the games we create and the live services that we offer, collectible digital content is going to play a meaningful part in our future".

NFT promises a level of interactivity in gaming that has been hitherto impossible, which is massively significant. This is a huge industry, worth billions; in fact worth more than the music and movie industries combined. The ascent of NFT in this niche is massive for cryptos, huge for blockchain, a game-changer for the whole digital currency space.

However, perhaps the most telling and profound indication of the cultural importance of the blockchain going forward came in a Bloomberg editorial, published on

2nd July, 2021. Bloomberg predicted that "everything will soon be on the blockchain", and headlined the article with a phrase that neatly sums up the impact of the crypto rush, and the entire theme of this book.

Bloomberg simply wrote...the future is decentralized.

Printed in Great Britain
by Amazon